NEPTUNE'S REVENGE

Also by Anne W. Simon:

The Thin Edge: Coast and Man in Crisis
No Island Is an Island: The Ordeal of Martha's Vineyard
The New Years: A New Middle Age
Stepchild in the Family

ANNE W. SIMON

NEPTUNE'S REVENGE
The Ocean of Tomorrow

FRANKLIN WATTS　1984
NEW YORK · TORONTO

Library of Congress Cataloging in Publication Data

Simon, Anne W.
Neptune's revenge.

Bibliography: p.
Includes index.
1. Marine pollution.   2. Marine resources conservation.
I. Title.
GC1085.S55   1984   333.91'64   84-11803
ISBN 0-531-09761-7

To a safe ocean for
Andy, Cathy, Eli, Ben,
Nick, Andrea, Benn Stuart,
Rebecca, Jessica, and Sarah

Acknowledgments

This book's value depends upon the precision of its facts. I am therefore immensely grateful for the critical scientific review given these pages by Dr. Robert Howarth of the Marine Biological Laboratory at Woods Hole and Editor-in-Chief of the new international scientific journal *Biogeochemistry*. Experts in other areas reviewed specific chapters. Thanks for these helping hands to: Dr. William Brown, Environmental Defense Fund; Sarah Chasis, Natural Resources Defense Council; Clifton Curtis, Oceanic Society; Professor Louis Henkin, Columbia University Law School; and Rafe Pomerance, Friends of the Earth. Many knowledgeable people talked to me about their particular sphere of ocean interest. I am indebted to all of them; their insights enrich this effort to present a succinct view of a vast subject.

My everlasting thanks for unswerving support of this book's concept and contents to my esteemed friend and agent, Dorothy Olding. Thanks, too, to this volume's editor, Ellen Joseph, to Ina Fine for the gift of time to write it, and to Rose Carrano, expediter superior. Research assistance provided by Sonia Sheldon and Dr. Roberta Weisbrod, *seriatim*, made it possible to complete this book in something short of a lifetime.

My ultimate gratitude is to my husband Walter Werner who lent this volume his admirable intellect and its author his unfailing interest and patience beyond the imaginable.

Contents

NEPTUNE'S REVENGE

Prologue

At a pause in a cruise among the Galapagos Islands, those black rock outcroppings shimmering in the equatorial sun off Ecuador, children jumped overboard where a herd of sea lions were swimming. The slim tanned bodies raced to catch up with the big-eyed, chunky sea lions, members of the suborder of pinnipeds, seals and walrus. Soon they mixed together, the sea lions executing graceful turns and dives, the splashing children shouting with excitement. Both species appeared marvelously stimulated by each other.

Watching them in the water side by side was remarkably moving. I wondered if they were celebrating a prehistoric togetherness, some tie that might have existed before pinnipeds, along with other mammals, left the land for life in the ocean, millions of years past. Was it a flashback allowed me into the mysterious attachments of an earlier world, or was it, perhaps, a hint of the future of *Homo sapiens?*

Below this place, down in the black ocean depths, is the Galapagos Rift, a tear in the earth's crust discovered in the late 1970s. Hot liquid from inside the planet spouts out into the darkness. Rich in hydrogen sulfide, it provides energy for sea-floor bacteria, among the oldest known life forms, and these, in turn, nourish a recently photographed colony of huge white clams, mussels, crabs, an unfamiliar genus of worms—the only known ecosystem independent of sunlight for its food supply. The liquid from the planet's interior

1

soon solidifies into ore, bearing great amounts of valued minerals, easily mined.

This primal process in the depths combined with the joyful meeting in the cobalt water above gave me a striking perspective. It was a shock to realize the millions upon millions of years that the ocean has existed in a more or less steady state and in what a microscopic speck of time—this half century—we have acquired the power to change the vast ancient domain. The reality so astounded me that it was impossible not to investigate what the changes are and how they have come about.

Faith in the infallible sea is strong, painful to surrender. I discovered this while working on a book about the coast and an earlier one about an island. Both coast and island had been transformed in our century. People crowded onto the coast, altered contours, developed harbors and shores, filled in wetlands, concretized dunes. They used the coast as if there were no tomorrow, only this chance to take advantage of the shore for their particular purposes. Change in the whole was unrecognized. Each new use was seen as separate and urgent.

The power to change the coast is based on compromise, something for everybody. The coast should be protected and developed—an impossible dream—is the formula. The result is a coast that can no longer shelter fish in its estuaries or keep land dry behind it or even retain sand on most of its beaches and dunes, a coast where the natural state is already irretrievable.

We are somehow surprised by the coast's deterioration, the sewage-strewn beaches, poisoned fish, overcrowded harbors. It is hard to believe that in our wisdom we made this happen, but it is true, we did. The coast is vulnerable to our use. It suffers from our inability to respect it.

The power to change the ocean, arriving some decades later, magnifies the coast experience. All over the world, people are making new use of the ocean and the ocean responds by change. These changes are just beginning to be understood, some just even beginning to be noticed. Scientists pursue them within relatively new specialties. The ocean does not yet yield neat bundles of statistics and absolute facts on the state of its health. It is too soon. But as I add together information from a dozen disciplines, unmistakable trends loom large.

The ocean has suffered from these few years of man's intervention. It has deteriorated. Its systems are degenerating, its species disappearing. Parts of the sea are dying, spreading disease as they perish; parts are too poisoned to support a healthy ecosystem. No one is certain whether ocean functions are retrievable or ocean deterioration is reversible. No one knows how close we are to ocean disaster.

Leading scientists agree that the process of deterioration toward disaster will continue over many years, leaving us a time margin between now and then. Studying the effects of our ocean uses and the poignant efforts of man to take over from nature the management of the sea, I have come to realize the poverty of minds to which we entrust the ocean and the urgent need to use whatever time we may have to deal with its fundamentals.

The big story of this book is not only that new uses of the ocean have set us in a dangerous direction but that there is an alternative. The record itself, documented in the next pages, has the strength to galvanize us to seize this alternative. We will not sit by, satisfied with vintage ideas about the deep and dark-blue ocean, while it is ravaged, its ecosystems trembling toward dysfunction. The facts assembled here urge us to undertake a momentous, radical course by which we can rescue the necessary ocean and keep it safe.

1
TO RISK THE SEA

When the whirling earth cooled from its molten begin-
nings, water seeped out of it to collect in the globe's rough rock
basins. The earth has had an ocean ever since. This ocean is necessary to existence. From its thin expanding floor in the dark, quiet
deep to its surface nutrient broth warming in the sun, the ocean
takes care of a goodly share of the earth's business. Joined with air
and land, it makes this the planet of life.

The ancients had a powerful god who ruled the sea, Neptune
to the Romans, Poseidon to the Greeks. He carried his trident, a
three-pronged spear, everywhere, used it to keep order in his domain. He could shatter rocks with his trident, call forth or subdue
storms, shake the shore into place. It is said that he created the
horse, and that his own golden-maned horses drew his chariot over
the sea which became calm before him as he kept his empire in
shape. The god was the invincible protector of the mysterious
kingdom, the marvelously energetic, productive, beautiful sea.

The control that was Neptune's has been seized by our society, first in history with the power to intrude on the sea and by
intruding change its ways. Expanding numbers in the world want
more and more of the ocean's resources, more fish for protein, more
oil from undersea rock, more minerals, more room to get rid of
growing piles of waste, be it toxic chemicals, radioactive discards,
or sewage.

Our trident is technology. It makes these new uses of the ocean
possible.

We use the ocean as we always have, freely, confidently. But what we use it for has changed. Although we have had a surfeit of warnings in the last decades that the new uses are damaging the ocean, we cling to the now-false comfort of taking the ocean for granted. In this we are shamelessly encouraged by industrial interests which race to harvest ocean riches before society detects the harm thus inflicted.

New ocean uses that technology engenders threaten ocean systems. Digging for oil on the Outer Continental Shelf risks suffusing the ocean with petroleum hydrocarbons. Some of the killing effects of these compounds on creatures of the sea are already documented. Some are known but smothered by the industry that would have us believe that oil and water are a healthy mix. Abilities to overfish, sweeping the sea, are out of control. Species fail; some disappear from the globe. Others are poisoned by one form or another of toxic waste we dump into the ocean.

Most difficult of all is to adjust the mind to slow ocean time. The ocean moves its great bulk very slowly and change within it is correspondingly slow. On the cold heavily pressured sea floor, growth is so slow that a certain fish, recently discovered, only reaches sexual maturity at age fifty, a clam at age two hundred.

At this leisurely pace, sea floor organisms take an inordinate time (from our fast-moving, impetuous view) to react to the toxics we dump in the ocean miles above their home base. Such dumping is still acceptable practice. Those who endorse it say there is no proof of change so no cause for concern. Most toxic chemical compounds have a killing record; this record plus ocean time predicts what is to come. Generally, however, such sober reasoning is ignored.

Power to change the sea could be the most momentous event in all man's years, and it has just begun. I remember Rachel Carson's statement in 1950 that "man cannot control or change the ocean . . . as he has subdued and plundered the continents," and how startled I was that changes familiar in the 1980s were unanticipated by this expert such a few years before. She had thought it could never happen, that the sea was impervious to whatever creatures walked the earth and whatever they chose to do, and ocean watchers of her time agreed.

Symbolically, an all-wise, all-protective Neptune still guarded the health of the ocean in the minds of distinguished scientists and of ordinary people in the 1950s. Each of us had the security of knowing that the ocean was there, intact, as it always had been and always would be, a fact of life so basic that it was hardly mentioned, any more than the tree in the garden, the blue sky, or the sun. An occasional view of the ocean, a swim, a sail, reinforced the comfort of an everlasting sea. We took for granted a sea that supports ships and shelters fish in all their variety, free for man to use as he requires. It was a pattern securely woven into the tapestry of human experience. For all too many, it is still believed intact.

Fascination with ocean processes is as old as stargazing and much more lively. The immense ocean systems produced gigantic storms, towering waves, tides that seemed to connect to the moon, great varieties of fish and shellfish which made their home in the ocean. Our ancient forebears were intrigued, their deductive capacities stimulated to puzzle out the complexities of the ever-changing sea.

The ancients had a consummate interest in the sea. Alexander the Great was perhaps inspired by Aristotle, a knowledgeable ecologist and Alexander's teacher until age sixteen. Alexander's marine interest long survived him, being noted by Roger Bacon in the thirteenth century: "Machines can be made for walking in the sea and rivers, even to the bottom without danger." Bacon says, "For Alexander the Great employed such, that he might see the secrets of the deep. . . ." An intriguing sixteenth-century Indian miniature shows Alexander being lowered into the water some distance from shore in a large glass barrel from which he was happily observing the denizens of the deep. On the surface, several boats hover, crowded with courtiers, some holding ropes to the barrel, some praying, some chatting as though this was an everyday affair. Perhaps it was.

A century earlier, Herodotus, in his history of Greece, noted petrified seashells in the hills, surrounded by salt. He concluded that these places must have once been covered by seawater.

He was right, although he could not have guessed that what he saw was a remnant of one of the four great glaciations which have taken place in the last billion years. Each time water is pulled into ice, it lowers the sea level from 100 to 500 meters; the level rises again when the ice melts. Since the process takes 10,000 to 20,000 years, Herodotus, living in an interglacial time of an ice age, as we do, saw the remains of an era when water, unfrozen, was at a higher level. Old coastlines wander through U.S. hills, too. A keen eye can detect ancient shells, even the remains of sand dunes, standing golden in the forest.

This scrap of information fits into a broad view of the globe, now visible for the first time. We can detect the still dim outline of the globe's evolution, of how it sustains itself, of the interaction between earth and ocean that forever recycles essentials for life. A discovery of the 1960s—continental drift and the spreading sea floor—is a breakthrough in earth sciences. Revolutionary in application, it can explain the amazing global system, but merits only a short digest in this volume, where the purpose is to describe how man has changed the sea in these few short years.

The earth is about 4.6 billion years old, the ocean about 2.5 billion years old. The conviction, strongly reconfirmed in the last several years, is that the ocean's water came from gases inside the rocky earth by a process of "degassing." Most degassing took place early in the world's history, Professor Thomas Schopf, of the University of Chicago, says in *Paleoceanography*. If, as some believe, it is still continuing, the amount is so slight as to be unmeasurable and there are an astounding 318 million cubic miles of water in the ocean. Schopf says: "The volume of the ocean has been in a steady state for the past 2.5 billion years."

During the eons of its existence, the ocean has been a theater of action. A colossal mid-ocean ridge thrust up from the sea floor to encircle the globe beneath the waves, occupying a third of the floor. Hot rock from inside the globe emerges through the ridge's valley, spreads out, pushing the sea floor before it until the old floor's edges collide with continental margins. The floor is then shoved into deep trenches, some deeper than several Grand Canyons, to be recycled inside the earth. Thus the sea floor is newer and thinner than continental rock, being constantly replaced. It is divided into seven tectonic plates which move throughout the ocean floor, bearing the continents.

The Americas are moving west at 2.5 centimeters a year. (10 cm = 3.9 inches.) Most of the Pacific moves east at 7.5 centimeters a year. Australia, India, and Saudi Arabia go north at 5 to 6 centimeters a year. These same plates tore apart Pangaea, the first primitive landform, some 200 million to 135 million years ago, separating it into enough continents so that residents can battle with each other over who owns what. There being no people around then, nature split Pangaea as it saw fit, and the ocean filled the spaces in between.

Then came mankind and the romance of man's relation with the sea. In the richness of that alliance, humans were inspired to poetry, imagery, curiosity that still sends children scurrying into the shallows to watch snails make their slow sure way up a rock and crabs scuttle along a sandy bottom. The sea might be the scene of a rapturous fisherman, of the heady victory of a scientist, defining the effect of oil on microscopic plankton after years of patient measurements. Such energizing, stimulating ocean experiences press us on to know more.

Even in his old age, Ulysses, as Lord Tennyson imagined him, master navigator and lifelong adventurer on the seas, looks for one more opportunity:

Some work of noble note, may yet be done,
Not unbecoming men that strove with Gods.
The lights begin to twinkle from the rocks:

The long day wanes: the slow moon climbs: the deep
Moans round with many voices. Come, my friends,
'Tis not too late to seek a newer world,
Push off, and sitting well in order, smite
The sounding furrow: for my purpose holds
To sail beyond the sunset, and the baths
Of all the Western stars, until I die.

From the ancients forward, the contagious effort to understand the sea persists. Saltiness, for example, was a puzzlement in the fifth century B.C., when certain Greeks thought the sea was the sweat of the earth, therefore salty. Aristotle believed the sun evaporated surface water leaving the heavier salt behind. A three-year-old thinks salt in the sea comes from the shiny spout of a round container in the kitchen. It actually comes from the earth's crust, either washed down from the mountains or up from the ocean floor.

It is amazing to contemplate that seawater salinity has stayed more or less the same for the past half-billion years, as far back as can reasonably be measured. Even more amazing is that the relationship of one element to another in the water has also stayed nearly the same. The amounts may vary but the proportions do not.

Curiosity that urged pursuit of the matter of salt extends to tides, currents, waves, storms, to the ocean's depths and shallows, its flora and fauna, its circulation. To discover the reason for the sea's capricious nature has required the thought of many generations. Very gradually, over the centuries, the sea begins to be revealed.

Ocean use pushed impatiently against the bounds that had kept it within reach of primitive navigation. Trade and expansion urged the building of seaworthy ships. Seamanship was encouraged by men like Prince Henry the Navigator, fourth son of the king of Portugal, who established a mariners' school and at whose bidding, chart makers, astronomers, and travelers pooled observations. When the "Armchair Navigator" died in the mid-fifteenth century, Portuguese mariners had taken over many offshore islands and sailed down the West African coast. Pressures to move out to the larger world, to "smite the sounding furrow," were irresistible.

Use of the ocean and curiosity about it combined in men who burst from the southwest corner of Europe in the fifteenth century, set on discovery of the sea and lands beyond. The famed Iberian navigators—Columbus, Vasco da Gama, Balboa, Magellan—backed by their royal patrons, made fast work of locating routes to the world abroad. It was not long before societies all over the world were joined by ships, adventuring, pirating, trading, warring, fishing, and transporting passengers from place to place.

Pilgrim settlers relied on their ships for survival. They had to trade and could not move long distances on land through the thick forests which grew to the water's edge. They traveled by ships. By the end of the eighteenth century, New England enjoyed its golden age of maritime prosperity. In Salem, Massachusetts, shipowner Elias Hasket Derby, so wealthy that he was called "The King," had a sea school, its students recruited from the best families in town. The students' first voyage was at age fourteen. They retired at age thirty, having made a sizable fortune, a tradition which was passed along to sons and nephews. Derby's men were well known for a "combination of superlative seamanship and keen business acumen," a contemporary account says.

The more the sea was used, the more men of the sea and men of science became curious about it. As early as 1666, the Royal Society of London published *Directions for Sea-Men, Bound for Far Voyages* in which the Society directed sailors to keep an exact diary so that scientists could "study nature rather than books." The seamen were instructed "To remark carefully the Ebbings and Flowings of the Sea: To take Notice of the Nature of the Ground in all Soundings whether it be Clay, Sand, Rock: To observe the Declination of the Compass. . . ." This information gave scientists some new material, albeit secondhand.

It remained for the nineteenth-century desire for a transatlan-

13

tic ocean-floor cable to again persuade the Royal Society to examine the ocean's depths. For the first time the world learned that the bottom of the sea, thought a dead place, was exceedingly lively. The Royal Society's famous expedition on the H.M.S. *Challenger* circled the globe from 1872 to 1876. Its findings filled sixty volumes, a watershed in ocean science.

By mid-twentieth century, modern oceanography was underway. Suddenly, new resources are discovered by satellites high in the atmosphere, by men in diving capsules down in deep canyons, by intensified search of virgin areas. Almost overnight, there is oil available in the frozen Arctic, abundant tiny krill, food for whales, available in the frozen Antarctic. In a few years almost every ocean resource has come within the reach of the spectacular trident of our technology.

Only the ocean ecosystem gets in the way. At the very poles of the globe and in the sea between, we risk the ocean of tomorrow.

The ocean has no constituency. No society lives there to protect its house and garden, to be moved by the passion of territorial imperative to undertake ocean defense. Our government relegates the ocean to a bureaucracy assigned to a corner of the U.S. Department of Commerce, a bitterly revealing choice. Efforts to defend the ocean are put forward by a few men in Congress and a few hardworking environmental groups, not much more. No "work of noble note," such as Ulysses reached for, is anywhere to be seen.

On the contrary, as 1984 began, some scientists found seaweed with radioactive levels between 100 and 1,000 times higher than normal in the Irish Sea, offshore a nuclear-fueled reprocessing plant. Such radioactivity spreads through the ocean.

Under present pressures, marine life, already diminishing, will deteriorate further, become less valuable to man. Then life on earth, deprived of ocean support, will also deteriorate. Neptune will have his revenge.

This worst-case scenario is predicated on today's facts. It is a long-range forecast of how the entire ocean will react to our new uses. If there is a chance that we are bringing about an ocean holocaust—and the facts add up to more than an idle chance that this is so—then we must do what we can, now, to reverse it. All too quickly, the whole may be as irreversible as some of its parts already are.

In some ways this charge resembles consideration of the nuclear threat. "Each of us is called on to do something that no member of any generation before us had to do," Jonathan Schell, author of *The Fate of the Earth*, writes in *The New Yorker*, "to assume responsibility for the continuation of our kind—to *choose* human survival." The conscious choice, Schell says, is complicated by the fact that "we are able to respond to it (the nuclear threat) only before it happens."

Equally, this generation has to choose the sea's survival—which, as with the rest of the biosphere, is linked to mankind's survival—now. If ocean deterioration becomes irreversible, we lose. Unlike the nuclear bomb, disaster will come slowly, as far as is now known, one bit at a time. It has started with such as Atlantic salmon, striped bass, Chesapeake Bay, beloved of sailors and watermen, the Mediterranean, its disease-bearing waters now suffusing Neptune's home realm.

To risk the ocean is to risk ourselves, our children, our world.

15

2
THE SALMON LEGACY

The wild fish of the sea in all their marvelous variety are, for the first time ever, profoundly affected by man. We are still hunters in the ocean wilderness, relishing the catch and the eating thereof, taking whatever we can capture from the sea and using it to our advantage, as did the first primitive fishermen. In this crowded technological age, man encroaches on fish as never before. The results, it is widely agreed, are not good, but it is beyond the present ability to measure precisely how bad, how dangerous, how close to disaster. Gambling, we escalate our intrusion into the fish world.

Fish existence in the ocean is one of the wonders of the world. Billions of fish of some 30,000 species find the right food, temperature, depth, and living space to sustain continuity of birth, reproduction, and death, their remains being neatly recycled. There is a fish for every ocean niche, the result of an evolution that started when the ocean itself was forming and the first fish—first vertebrate on the planet—appeared in the primal mud, 430 million years ago. Over eons some species became extinct, new ones developed, their bodies refining to make ever more efficient use of their environment. Modern fish are the pinnacle, so far, of the torturously slow progress.

These denizens of the ocean, free-swimming fish, bottom-crawling shellfish, have long been considered an everlasting global resource. "All the great sea fisheries are inexhaustible," Dr. Thomas Huxley, renowned British biologist, told a London assemblage in the 1880s. "Nothing we can do can seriously affect the numbers of fish." The late historian Arnold Toynbee thought fish "a sure guarantee for our race's survival." He believed the sea would eventually contribute more food than the land. It was hard, then, to see around the corner.

In twenty-five years, natural processes have been forcibly interrupted. Man becomes the agent of change, altering fish environment, balance of numbers and species. It has happened too fast for fish to adapt, even if adaptation is possible. With the advent of our generation, it turns out that ocean bounty is not boundless after all.

The freckle-faced kid with pole and can of bait is going to have to change his expectations. More seriously, so are most hungry people. Change comes just when the world needs more fish. Fish provides necessary animal protein equal to that of most meat, and in a recent year supplied the world with about a third of the total, twice as much as eggs, three times as much as poultry. As the human population grows toward five billion or more, sources of these body-building amino acids must grow accordingly if human strength and health are to continue.

The effort to catch more fish succeeded at first. The world take was 4 million metric tons in 1900. Between 1950 and 1970 the catch zoomed from 21 million metric tons to 70 million. Vested interests, wanting to keep on fishing, predicted 100 million tons by the year 2000. But by the late '60s and early '70s, most experts knew the truth. Overfishing had already had disastrous effects. By the 1980s, the statistics proved them right. The world catch levels were off, just barely increasing, even with vastly more effort, and there is doubt that even the present catch level will continue, given changing ocean conditions.

A strong current of trouble and deprivation surfaces. Striped bass, sport fishing favorites, are at a twenty-five-year low. Backbones weakened by PCB and other chemicals in their bodies, their ability to chase food, and to defend themselves against predators,

20

slows. The species is depleted. In some offshore waters, shellfish are carcinogenic; elsewhere, lobsters languish. On Georges Bank off Massachusetts, a principal international fishery, Atlantic herring, one of the world's most abundant food fish, has virtually disappeared. The herring catch, a colossal 373,000 metric tons in 1968, plummets to 1,700 metric tons in 1980. On a recent cruise to the Bank where herring once swarmed, three were found.

We begin to get some idea of the enormity of the task of keeping fish in the sea. Whether the present society can do it, or will do it, is unpredictable. Requirements of this undertaking are to understand what fish need and to be willing to give it to them. The enigma, the challenge, the sacrifices required, are sometimes combined and brilliantly lit by a particular fish, able to arouse both affection and primal predatory emotions in man. Such is the case in the fate, after several thousand years of existence, of the renowned Atlantic salmon.

Ecstasies of battle with the noble salmon, flashing silver in a dark pool, arching in a jump to the sun, make fishermen the world over passionate in defense of this most desirable prey. "I desperately want to see the salmon survive as a species," HRH Prince Charles tells an assemblage, citing the "excitement, tranquility and appalling despair" the fish has given him. Centuries before, King William passed laws to protect salmon in Scotch rivers, and centuries before that, Caesar's legions discovered the fish swarming in the rivers of Gaul, named it *Salmo salar*, *Salmo* from the Latin to leap, *salar* from the Latin root for salt.

Through time the salmon has been much honored. The male, complete with the hooked jaw it shows in spring and summer, appears in Ice Age cave paintings in France and Spain, c. 25,000 to 10,000 B.C.. Salmon decorates Glasgow's heraldic coat of arms, and three slender fish are the emblem of Mandel, a Norwegian town on a once-renowned salmon river where there is now not a *Salmo salar* to be seen.

The salmon's life makes it extraordinarily vulnerable to hu-

21

man interference, so much so that one investigator calls it "a valuable indicator organism. Its well-being," he says, "is one of the best guarantees for a healthy environment." And, he implies, the reverse is true as well. Until recently the salmon's life pattern was unchanging. An anadromous fish, it lives in freshwater and salt, is spawned on clean gravel high in a fast-flowing river where it spends its first years gaining strength enough to migrate to the ocean. Here it travels as far as 2,000 miles from home, its destination, unknown for many centuries, discovered just a few years ago. It goes to the open ocean to feed, and when ready to spawn, miraculously finds its river again. No one yet knows that secret of its navigation. Some say it is by the stars, some believe the great fish can smell or taste its river's special chemicals or feel its currents. Accurate and determined, it summons all its considerable strength to fight its way upriver against the current, climbing fish ladders, leaping waterfalls, avoiding all hazards to be able to spawn in the spot where it was born.

Atlantic salmon probably migrated across the Arctic at some distant time, leaving a close relative, the steelhead trout, and the more distant Pacific salmon family to colonize west coast waters. *Salmo salar* thrived on both sides of the Atlantic through the centuries. There are tales that it was once so plentiful that when gathered at a river's mouth, waiting to go upstream to spawn, the crowds of fish were so dense that wagons could be driven across the river on their backs. Salmon was scorned as a common fish; there are records of employer guarantees that workers would not be forced to eat it more than twice a week.

Salmon became a source of sport as well as food when gentlemen anglers around the northern hemisphere discovered its courageous hard-fighting nature and made the fish the center of a vigorous cult. In mid-nineteenth century, when salmon started to decline, anglers formed societies, conducted research, had laws passed, all concentrated on protecting salmon. They tried to guard the lordly fish against apparent problems—predators, despoiled habitats, overfishing. Hunger for the hunt and admiration for the hunted were motives as strong as commercial fishermen's gain.

Salmon protectors ran headlong into gray seal protectors in Scotland where most of the world's gray seals live and where, in 1914, seals had dwindled to a mere 500 individuals. They are powerful salmon predators, along with porpoises, otters, minks, owls, eagles. Nevertheless the Scots passed a law for seal survival. By 1963 there were 30,000 seals. This population explosion among salmon predators caused a salmon decline, inciting the fish's protectors to urge reestablishment of legal gray seal killing. In the 1970s, that again became the law of the land.

By what Jovian reference could man decide—seals or salmon? As the issue intensifies, one must wonder whether we can ever know enough to choose between one species or another, or to choose the fate of a single species.

Evolution is now subject to conscious control, George Gaylord Simpson, scientist, says. Man is qualified for the job by reason of "the accumulation of knowledge, the rise of a sense of values." The reassuring thought is punctured by facts. We are rapidly moving away from the position of a richly diverse biosphere with possibilities for unlimited biological expansion. The world is losing species at a rate between forty and 400 times as fast as in eons past, Anne and Paul Ehrlich say in *Extinction:* "Perhaps as much as one-fifth of all species on earth today will have vanished by the end of the century."

Do we know enough to build the sense of values that will protect the earth? In the growth society, it is hard to even identify decisions, much less make them with wisdom.

This was the case in another choice—fish or development— that plagued salmon devotees. The Crown owned all fishing rights in the United Kingdom and began protecting the salmon habitat as early as the year 996 when Ethelred II forbade the sale of young fish. In 1318 the Crown ordered nets at the river's mouth spaced far enough apart for a sow and her pigs to pass. This so-called King's

Gap was to give fish easy access to the river. By the mid-nineteenth century, protection extended to gravel in spawning beds, making it an offense to remove gravel, a requirement to replace it. A Royal Commission found overfishing and river obstruction the chief reasons for salmon decline, and suggested remedies. Nevertheless, the most prolific salmon river, the Tees, had no fish by 1940 and another, the Tyne, fell from 17,000 fish to nil by 1959. Dams, power plants, water-cooled industry, and pollution increased on rivers on both sides of the Atlantic. Salmon decreased, despite lifts and ladders installed for their convenience. From the Hudson east to Maine's Penobscot, rivers produced power, but no salmon.

Earnest efforts to clean up rivers recently attracted a brave *Salmo salar* 15 miles upstream from London Bridge, first in the Thames for 160 years, and another loner into the Hudson amid cheers and optimistic headlines. In the Connecticut River, a fifteen-year-old restoration program includes a million-dollar fishway that lets salmon cross a 12-foot-wide dam. This, plus hatchery stock added to the river, lured some 500 fish in 1981.

Overfishing has always plagued salmon and fishermen. How much is enough to capture? The guessing game—and it still is a guess—is under way. Its question arouses passion among anglers, so much so that an early Scotch king, Robert III, ordered death to anyone taking a salmon out of season. "The remarkable bounty of Scotland's natural salmon rivers will be steadily destroyed by man's shortsighted selfishness," a fisherman says at a recent Edinburgh symposium. "The greed of man increases with each passing year," a Canadian comments. "That the Atlantic salmon has survived until now is a miracle." For a century there have been laws in most countries to control the salmon catch so that the remaining stock will be large enough to regenerate itself. Regulations are haphazard, difficult to police. Poaching and illegal fishing persist.

Overfishing flourishes by netting salmon on their migration routes to winter hideouts in the ocean. The Irish are particularly fond of "drift netting" the salmon from many nations en route, a practice which doubled their harvest in the 1960s and '70s, "an example of rake's progress," an official of the Salmon and Trout Association says. In 1956, a salmon tagged from a British river was caught off West Greenland . . . and the hitherto sacred (to salmon) international feeding grounds were discovered.

Every nation with a fishing boat rushed to scoop up the bounty. The annual salmon catch jumped from 64 tons to 2,300 tons in a few years, quickly reflected by declining runs in home rivers. In 1969 an international ban on drift netting and fishing in the feeding grounds was accepted by most nations. In 1981 a treaty was signed that outlaws salmon fishing in the ocean altogether, limiting catch to "the country of origin." The core question—how much is enough—remains unsolved.

The irony of man's long love affair with *Salmo salar* is that the species is about to perish by pollution from heaven, a product of man's own making. The new murderous trouble is acid rain which pours into rivers of the Northwest and Canada. Salmon is particularly sensitive to acid; reproduction falters, embryos fail to hatch or if they do, produce infant fish with pathological alterations severe enough to kill or forever maim them. The acid is sulfur dioxide and nitric acid, much of it from Midwest power plants and from automobile exhaust, combining in the air to collect in the clouds, be blown east to rain down into the salmon's crucial reproductive environment.

The scenario has played elsewhere. Acid rain was discovered in the 1960s when salmon in the famous fishing rivers of Norway and Sweden declined and river acidity increased. By the '70s there were no fish at all, a change attributed by scientists to acid rain, arriving by cloud from industrialized Western Europe. Short of international agreement, there was nothing that Scandinavia could do. Canada experiences the same swift deadly salmon decline. In Nova Scotia, one hundred-year records show the catch holding steady until 1950. Today the nine most acidic rivers have no salmon; in others, fish are decreasing. It takes fifteen to twenty years from the first trouble signs to salmon extinction, Canadian authorities say. They identify half of Canada's acid rain as made in the United States.

U.S. salmon cannot stay out of the rain. As rivers east of Maine's Penobscot become more acidic, salmon diminish. Palliative measures such as liming lakes and streams are temporary at best. To be in time to save *Salmo salar*, we would have to stop made-in-America acid rain, fast. Legislation for this purpose started through Congress in 1981 but was put aside by the Reagan administration in favor of "more study." The administration, believing the acid rain tag "too emotional," orders the rain in question to be called "poorly buffered precipitation," a high-level official says.

Most people do not want to surrender the remarkable fish that has accompanied man since the Ice Age. But neither will most people limit the industrial freedom that produces acid rain, the salmon's ultimate killer. Instead of adapting ourselves to salmon needs—unobstructed rivers, clean pure water, et al.—it is proposed that salmon adapt instead. Cornell University has already experimented with creating acid-tolerant brown trout and could proceed to try for the same result with salmon. Dr. Eville Gordon, biologist at the University of Minnesota, points out that if this science-fiction nightmare was brought about, the salmon would need food. Dr. Gordon continues, "To breed acid-tolerant food webs would, in my view, be an impossible task."

Another alternative is to remove the river from the salmon's life, substituting hatcheries in estuaries. This scheme has produced big-scale salmon ranching, mostly on the West Coast. Such excessive interference with nature begets a fascinating bit of new knowledge. The ocean, it appears, has a limited carrying capacity for salmon. It was discovered in Oregon where eager salmon ranchers, releasing 60 million coho smolts into the Pacific each year, found they got diminishing returns. By virtue of careful statistical studies, two scientists discovered that there was not enough food in the ocean to feed all the young coho. The coho spend their growing time competing for the food that is available, leaving themselves open to predators, starvation, and other natural disasters. The optimum number—the carrying capacity of the sea in this region—is found to be 44 million. At this level, more adult salmon survive. Overcrowding does not appear to work any better in the sea than it does on land.

By our actions we have judged the Atlantic salmon expendable. The instincts of the lordly fish which has fascinated man for so long are now diluted by new hatchery strains, bred to satisfy industrial demands. These new subspecies, interbreeding with whatever few wild fish survive acid rain, will from here forward diminish the compelling strength and determination in the unique gathering of genes that made *Salmo salar* legendary.

The legacy of this single species is to sharpen perception of the massive pressure we put on fish in the sea, pressure such as they have never known and, apparently, cannot abide.

3
IMPRUDENT PREDATORS

Every drop of ocean water contains a microscopic speck
that is alive. Minute plankton, produced with the sun's energy, float
in the sea to feed larger life forms. Plant plankton make animal
plankton possible. Animal plankton nourish ocean life, from bot-
tom-dwelling clams to whales that engulf millions of plankton in
one gulp. Of all of the ocean's resources, its living inhabitants are
invaluable for humans. And, perhaps more than we are, they are
essential to the survival of the biosphere.

The salmon's fate points to the radical change we are making
for marine life. Until we recognize the state of fish, we cannot know
much about the effects of other changes or arrive at judicious action.

Fish are the bellwether of sudden, awesome, and perhaps irreversible ocean change. Our pressure on fish is twofold. We change
their environment in ways equivalent to pouring acid into salmon
rivers, if somewhat less easily measured, a matter which occupies
the next chapter. Here the subject is the pressure of overfishing.

Going fishing—the words conjure up pleasant seashore scenes.
Children perched on the dock impatiently waiting to hook squid
which they sell to the local fish market for 25 cents a pound; an
angler casting from the beach in an expert arc, hauling in a massive bluefish; a fishing fleet chugging into a bay at dawn where "the
birds are working," a friendly avian alert to the piscian presence.
Romantic memories, all.

Going fishing has exploded into a different world. Now it means use of new wizardly abilities to locate and land fish by sonar, radar, and by amazing inventions which vacuum the bottom of the sea. It means harbors crowded with sleek white cruisers with wall-to-wall carpeting and capacious freezers for the catch. With increased capacity to catch fish and a burgeoning world population needing protein, we fish as though fisheries are, indeed, inexhaustible, as Huxley believed a century ago. But we are beginning to discover otherwise.

The direct approach—fish more to get more—no longer works as it did in simpler days. A dizzying example is the birth, growth, and collapse of the anchoveta fishery off the coast of Peru. Starting with just a few fish in the early 1950s, it increased ninety-fold in nine years to become the world's largest fishery. In 1970, over 12 million metric tons of anchovetas were captured in Peruvian waters, nearly a fifth of the world's total fish take. Birds living on offshore rocks fed off anchovetas; the bird droppings, guana found to be valuable fertilizer, and were soon the basis of a thriving Peruvian industry. Man's share of the anchoveta catch was converted into high-protein valued feed for poultry and pigs. It became Peru's number one export.

Twice, a limit of 9.5 million tons was proposed for the anchoveta catch; twice it was ignored, "like leaving your gigantic winnings on the table in a roulette game," an observer comments. In 1972 the catch plummeted to less than half; in 1980 it was only .72 million tons. There has been no significant recovery, no more winnings from the sea for Peru. Some talk persists that an unusual change in *El Nino*, the Peruvian coastal current, might have been responsible, but overfishing is more often charged with the disaster.

An earlier dramatic forebear of this crash was the collapse of the fifty-year-old Pacific sardine fishery in the 1940s. This immense fish source inspired its first cannery in 1889. By the 1930s there were eighteen processing plants in Monterey, California, center of the sardine business and setting for John Steinbeck's *Cannery Row:*

> In the morning when the sardine fleet has made a catch, the purse-seiners waddle heavily into the bay blowing their whistles. Then cannery whistles scream and all over town men and women scramble into their clothes and come running down to go to work. The whole street rumbles and groans and screams and rattles while the silver rivers of fish pour in out of the boats. . . .

At the height of the fishery in 1936, 800,000 tons of fish streamed from seventy-eight specially designed boats (named purse-seiners for their particular nets) into the cans of Monterey. This amazing yield lasted a few years, then tumbled. By 1953 there were only 10,000 tons and in 1967, somewhat too late to matter, California put a moratorium on sardine landings, even for bait. The fishery was over.

Seven billion sardines caught in 1939, a tenth of a billion in 1949—what happened? This is a much studied fishery. Even so, it was difficult, in those relatively unsophisticated days, to recognize and accept that the crash was coming. When the decline began, some said it was caused by the concurrent cooling of the Pacific; others believed the sardines had left the area. To support that theory, there is said to be fossil evidence that sardines undergo cycles of abundance of 500 to 1700 years around the world, spending just a short time on America's West Coast. "The Pacific sardine is not disappearing," two scientists state in 1951. "The decline is due to . . . poor spawning seasons." Today, although more is known about what fish need to survive, the matter is still debated. It is thought that overfishing might have accelerated the natural cycle and caused the crash.

Halibut were overfished in mid-nineteenth century because it was not yet known that the females become sexually mature only at age nine or ten. The nubile females looked big enough to catch but were, in truth, virgins, hope of the future. The developing appetite for halibut in Boston supported immense catches, including the mothers-to-be. Soon waters once alive with halibut produced but a few, a condition which still prevails.

Haddock, herring, flounder, lobsters, surf clams . . . all overfished. Even cod, a staple for primitive man thousands of years ago, the fish that lured the Vikings to these shores, has succumbed. Centuries ago, swarming cod, and haddock too, on the shallow Banks off New England and Newfoundland, drew fishing boats over the sea to fill their holds with food for Catholic Europe. No matter how many pregnant boats creaked their way back across the Atlantic, these fisheries continued to be productive. Cod· was important to the economy, being the foundation of the so-called Golden Triangle. Ships loaded with salted cod sailed to Spain, where it was sold; then to Africa, where cod money bought slaves; across the sea to the West Indies, where slaves were traded for sugar and molasses; and back to New England to sell these ingredients for rum.

The great cod fisheries in the northwest Atlantic seemed forever fertile. Each fish lays nine million eggs at a time (at least one in a million matures). In 1933, a reliable report says, a schooner in Alaska's Bering Sea caught 700 tons of cod, 453,365 fish, in a single day. But the once superabundant cod have been fished beyond limits. There is a growing shortage. Cod consumption rises 8 percent a year; cod landings increase not at all in the North Atlantic. According to biologists, there just are not any more cod available.

"There is some doubt that man can be a prudent predator," Richard Hennemuth, director of the Woods Hole Laboratory of the National Marine Fisheries Service says. The environment has a limited capacity to support a given population of fish. Kill too many and the remaining smaller numbers will produce more in order to catch up. Once this excess, too, has been killed, the decline it masked is revealed. Ergo, overfishing.

Stone Age man had no such troubles. It took courage, then, to become a predator of fish at all. The first evidence of using the sea as a source of food was found in South Africa; it was about 10,000 years old. To exist, man killed what he could reach with available weapons, probably spearing fish at first, then using a gorge, a stone wrapped in bait which stuck in the fish's gullet, then venturing to build a dugout canoe which would take him farther into the water.

Interestingly, when the Greeks colonized the coast and Aegean islands many millennia later, they had to learn from the Phoenicians to eat food from the sea, accustomed as they were to the flesh of wild animals. Fish, we are told, was a staple mainly of the very poor. In *The Iliad* and *The Odyssey*, no fish are described at banquets or in the houses of the rich. Homer has a few accounts of eating fish but even at sea, he says, meals seemed to consist of wine and meat, the latter most generally being stolen on various islands.

According to Plato, fishing was "not an occupation worthy of a man wellborn or well brought up, it not being the occasion of healthy exercise." By the Middle Ages, fishing emerges as big business. Large-scale fishing in fleets became a lucrative industry. It was the basis of the Hanseatic League, power of the North Sea, the rise of the Dutch and Portuguese fishing fleets and of the famous British fishing ports. "It is the fish taken upon His Majesty's coasts that is the only cause of the increase of shipping in Europe," Sir William Monson, an admiral in the reign of James I, remarks. Even so, in those earlier times the world catch was small compared to the present, and overfishing was not much in evidence.

The fishing industry in the United States was surprisingly small in the 1960s. There were 130,000 fishermen, 70,000 fishing boats, less than 2,000 processors, wholesalers, export-importers. Most boats were small, 80 percent individually owned, and there were just a few large companies. The total amount of the domestic catch stayed about the same from the mid-'40s to mid-'60s. Change showed up in species caught—less food fish, more fish for industrial use.

Then, with a suddenness that forced attention to the state of fish, fisheries, and fishermen, came what we might call the Piscian Revolution, an appropriately grand title for the first profound change in matters piscatorial since some brave native on an early shore took off in his canoe. The demand for fish jumped to unheard-of proportions. The method of catching fish was technologized beyond recognition, relegating hook, line, and sinker to history. The revolution produced the extraordinary capacity for fishing around the world in weeks. It inaugurated overfishing on a gigantic scale, change in species of fish and fishermen, and a bothersome global query—whose fish are they anyway?

World fish consumption doubled in the '50s and '60s. Fish for industrial use—fishmeal, fish oil, fertilizer—increased 700 percent. People were eating more fish because of habits of wartime meat rationing, economics—a fish dinner cost less in those days than steak—and real estate development, which displaced agriculture and cattle. Small-acreage Japan, for example, with less and less room to grow protein, hoped to take care of its exploding population's food needs from the sea. It led all nations in amount taken from global waters in 1980, a whopping 14 percent of the total, some 10,410,000 metric tons.

In the United States, the demand for fish grew twice as fast as the population. By 1980 the average American ate 13 pounds of fish in a year. These fish were a disproportionate share of the top of the line, worldwide—91 percent of the lobster landings, 46 percent of the scallops, 45 percent of the clams, and 41 percent of the tuna. Our national catch, not much increased over the years, is about 5 percent of the world catch, a third as much as Japan's. Sixty-five percent of the fish we eat is imported.

This is an odd circumstance since more than half of all fish caught in the world comes from the Atlantic northeast, Pacific northwest, and Pacific southeast, two of these most fertile areas being directly off U.S. coasts where most fish live, on or above the continental shelf. The Alice-in-Wonderland reversal which elevates our imports, springs from the revolution in fishing methods.

Hunting for fish is now performed with fast precision at the touch of a button. The newest scanning machines can locate even the smallest fish shoals, measure their size, depth, and direction. Cotton nets have given way to unbreakable nylon and, grown to gigantic size, are hauled by power-driven winches. To a degree, skill has become a matter of what you can afford. Until the '60s, tuna, for example, was landed by live-bait boats using poles and lines. Now equipment is a colossal floating computer. "Everything about a tuna superseiner is large," Michael Melzer says in his book about fishing methods. These giants may have a purse seine a mile long, helicopter landing platform, hydrocompass, radar set, ADF radios, a depth-sounder recorder. Most astonishing of all, one of these boats, the *Margaret I*, Melzer says, holds no less than 4 million pounds of tuna.

Enormous floating fish factories catch, process, and freeze what they have hauled and can keep the catch frozen for a year, "fresh-frozen," as restaurateurs call it. Foreign fishing fleets thus equipped moved into the rich fisheries off U.S. coasts in the 1960s. By 1970 there were hundreds such vessels on Georges Bank alone. The foreigners took fifty times the U.S. catch off the West Coast. On the Atlantic coast their catch was 94 percent of the total mackerel catch, 83 percent of the sea herring, 61 percent of the scallops.

Overfishing is just too easy for these giant fishing boats; in fact, it would be difficult to avoid. And this is a new kind of overfishing, five or six species at once, whatever happens to be in the neighborhood. Where the resulting fish decline used to take a decade, now it happens in one season. Five nations take most of the fish caught in the world and make most of the impact: Japan first, then the USSR, China, Norway, and the U.S., fifth. Developing countries—Thailand, Indonesia, the Philippines—are now impor-

37

tant fishing nations, too. At this writing the world catch stays about the same but requires more effort.

Evolution recedes. Earlier signs of change in species is now a full-blown trend. Some changes are caused by pollution of the ocean, as seen in the next pages, some by overfishing, but all appear to encourage fish lower in the food chain. "There is a decline in some of the most prized finfish species, such as the Atlantic cod and flounder," the Council on Environmental Quality reported to the president in 1981.

On Georges Bank, where herring vanished, an exploding population of sand lance have filled the herring niche, Dr. Kenneth Sherman at the Northeast Fisheries Center says. The newcomers are one of the opportunistic species which move into a vacuum and multiply exceedingly fast. They may be keeping herring and mackerel stocks low, Sherman says. Across the ocean, the Danes are making a big effort to use sand lance, which are also replacing herring off their shores, for fish meal. Here at home they are persistently regarded as "trash fish."

As species higher in the food chain continue to falter, the Revolution may bring about an ocean of trash fish. No one can predict its effects.

American settlers went fishing to feed the family and make a living selling the catch. The picturesque fisherman prototype is a literary cliché: a fiercely independent soul, blue eyes, weather-beaten face, yellow oilskins, owning his own boat, answering to nobody, who spends his days on the water dealing only with fish, wind, and weather. At the sign of occasional shortages of one species or another, he simply shifts operations to other grounds, other fish. "We think of fishermen as a group," Susan Peterson, anthropologist at Woods Hole Oceanographic Institution, says, "but they don't think of themselves that way nor see themselves as having an impact on presumably inexhaustible fisheries in the neighborhood. Their ultimate interest is in their own economies." Thus each contributes to overfishing, often without realizing it.

Fishing for fun, the ancient sport of angling, has also changed. "The angler is a contemplative person attuned to rural settings," Isaac Walton says in *The Compleat Angler* in mid-seventeenth century. Angling triumphs, he notes, are happy interludes for a man enjoying life's simple pleasures. The art of such fishing was the self-imposed handicap of equipment, requiring hard-earned skill; its motive, excellence. "A delicate cast," Walton says, "was good for nothing except the hooking of a single fish."

As a child I spent days watching my father angle for bonefish in a shallow southern bay. Crouched in a rowboat under the blazing sun, we waited for the telltale tail to cut through the water as the skittish, elusive fish, nose down, hunted for food. Total silence was the rule; it would be best, my father said, not to breathe very much. The reward for motionless, silent, sunburnt hours was the cast of a live shrimp just a foot or two ahead of the oncoming fish, its sudden snatch at the bait, the ensuing battle—bonefish are fierce fighters—and, if it happened, the victory.

This was pure sport. The fish, true to its name, is not good eating. Generally my father would measure it, admire it, and toss it back. But the catch remained in his mind to mark his skill. Next time, perhaps, he'd use an even lighter line, catch a bigger fish. . . .

The contemplative sport becomes competitive. Fish derbies reward the largest, the most. To win is no longer a private matter in a hidden bay but a contest between many fishermen and their equipment. Anglers buy bigger and bigger boats, the newest electronic fishing aids, and spend more and more money to go fishing.

Post–World War II, the crowd has quadrupled. At the start of the '80s there are between seventeen and twenty million sport fishermen landing perhaps as many edible finfish as the harvest of the approximately 200,000 U.S. commercial fishermen. "Direct expenditures of recreational fishermen have risen from $500 million in 1955 to approximately $5 billion in 1980," John Byrne, administrator of the National Oceanic and Atmospheric Administration (NOAA), says in 1982. Indirect contributions of sport fishing to the economy, he says, for food, lodging, gasoline, bait, far exceed the direct $5 billion. The total amount is necessarily a guess. Professor Julio Pontecarvo of Columbia University, an authority in ocean economy matters, puts the figure at $30 billion.

This gives sport fishermen considerable political clout. To the Reagan administration, their cash investment becomes more important than preserving the catch for which they invest. "We have adopted a new sport fishing policy," Byrne announces, "which departs from the tradition of considering primarily fish and habitat. It moves toward a more balanced approach that considers users and supporting industries. . . ." With the advent of legions of leisured fishermen, fish lose.

A fish taken by a recreational fisherman has ten times the value of the same fish commercially caught, Gil Radowski of the Sports Fishing Institute, a Washington-based pressure group, says, and the states believe it. Thus California recently designated striped bass as a recreation-only fish; Florida accords snook the same status, as Texas does for the fish called red drum. In New York City, striped bass were so valued that the building of Westway, a major highway system along the Hudson River, was condemned by the court in order to preserve bass spawning grounds. In Delaware, where all major fish species are less abundant, there is a decline in commercial fishing, a gradual takeover by sport fishermen.

There were not enough fish off U.S. shores in the 1970s to meet the demands of foreign fishing fleets, recreational fishermen, commercial fishermen. The remarkable rich natural resource of the ocean commons was diminished, edging toward the tragedy of most commons, but still in business. Competition was fierce.

Whose fish are they?

The United States answers, "Mine," and chases the colossal foreign fleets away. In 1976, Congress passed the Fishery Conservation and Management Act, known as the Magnuson Act for its chief architect. The law establishes a fishery zone 200 miles out into the water, giving the U.S. exclusive management of the fish in some 200 million square nautical miles—"the largest single pool of living resources possessed by any country in the world," the Department of Commerce says. About a fifth of the world's traditionally harvested marine fish are now claimed by the U.S.A. as its very own.

The new law sets up a bureaucracy to regulate fisheries "taking into account the social and economic needs of the states." The small phrase has a big impact. Translating governmentese, it means attention to the desires of big spenders: recreational fishermen, shoreline developers who would occupy estuaries where many fish live, oil companies digging offshore for the black gold that may lie hidden there.

The first gropings under the Magnuson Act are important insights into the larger confusion over ocean use, later considered. Suffice it to say that the plight of fish has not improved under new management.

The more we know about the fish and shellfish off our shores, the more difficult it becomes to live by the law we made to undertake their care. Revolutionary capacities for fishing shatter the idea of an inexhaustible supply of fish to eat, even of fish to catch for the fun of it. To curb the hunt for what has always been free for the taking, is a fundamental change in concept, not easily accepted. But the evidence is clear: fish cannot maintain any abundance with our kind of overfishing much longer.

The continuing existence of fish is newly threatened from another direction as well. Corrosion of their water world lessens chances for fish survival.

4

A SELECTION
OF POISONS

The ocean is home to all marine life, its land, air, source of food, its marriage bed, its grave. Species after species depend on the everlasting constancy of the ocean to survive. In our time and due to our intrusion, marine life can no longer rely on such constancy. We add great and unaccustomed amounts of matter to the ocean from the air shimmering above it, and from the land.

The ocean seems a likely place to get rid of the waste we make, big enough to handle whatever comes its way and possessing the happy ability to make it disappear with the flip of a wave. We cherish the fantasy that when waste vanishes from sight, it also vanishes from the planet.

Now that fantasy dissolves. Think of the ocean as one big lake and its newborn hazards are understandable. Scientists are discovering where waste goes beneath the waves, analyzing its effects on life in the sea and on man. Some of the substances we discard into the ocean interact with other elements to form puzzling new compounds. Some disintegrate into their parts, a process which itself is a stress on the big lake. Others do not decompose at all but are apparently taking up permanent residence in the sea. Because of slow ocean time, we cannot know what will happen until years into the twenty-first century. What we know now is that our wastes degrade the waters and catapult its inhabitants toward disaster.

Significant and well-scrutinized effects of waste illustrate. They suggest decisions to be made by the generation responsible for the fate of the ocean . . . ourselves.

Most basic of all impending catastrophies in the sea is the threat to plankton, single-cell ocean plants. Under the microscope, they look like silicate snowflakes in countless fantastic designs. These tiny delicate cells bear a profound burden. Phytoplankton (plant cells, in distinction to zooplankton, animals) are the foundation of the sea's food web. By photosynthesis, using the sun's radiant energy, they transform carbon dioxide, nutrients, and water into food for marine life.

The by-product of this spectacular natural process is oxygen. Some of it dissolves in the sea, where it is vital to the general metabolism, some goes into the air. Simplest of plants, these rootless unicells floating in the ocean may convert almost as much carbon dioxide to oxygen as all land plants combined.

Plankton were part of the ancient ocean system, their fossils dating back some 200 million years. They were first studied in mid-nineteenth century by Johannes Müller, a noted German zoologist. "When you have entered this pelagic magic world," Müller said, "you will not easily leave it again." Enchantment spread even to the renowned *Challenger* expedition, some years later, which found that plankton were not a local phenomenon but exist throughout the great blue expanse, a vast food crop riding the waves.

Just a few years ago, scientists at Woods Hole discovered miniature plankton growing in such profusion that they can account for a significant amount of the sea's biomass and perhaps much of its productivity. Never before detected, these are picoplankton, which hold just a trillionth of a gram of carbon each and are the size of about a thousandth of the period that ends this sentence. We are now equipped as never before to advance knowledge of these life-giving ocean plants. There are, for example, electronic devices which can count plankton numbers and diversity, accomplishing this painstaking work in minutes.

These little plants are furiously waving danger signals. They are intolerant of many man-made additions to the ocean, acids, for example, and oil. DDT and PCB are acutely toxic to them, perhaps more so to the larger than the smaller forms. There need be only twenty-five parts per billion of DDE, a DDT derivative, in the water to inhibit plankton's photosynthesis and cell division causing lower densities in at least one phytoplankton species, NOAA reports to Congress in 1980. PCB shifts the composition of the phytoplankton community in favor of smaller forms; so do other chemicals.

This is no minor event. Smaller phytoplankton may encourage smaller zooplankton which encourage small fish and jelly fish that can comfortably eat them. Harvestable fish may prefer large phytoplankton and cannot do well with small sizes; nor can shellfish, menhaden, and other filter feeders. The change in plankton size may diminish the entire ecosystem, although this is hotly debated among scientists.

Out in the great indigo spaces, the sea's meadows, ocean dwellers from miscroscopic zooplankton to bulky whales graze on the infinitesimal plants. Back in 1969 two scientists predicted that ocean plankton would be more vulnerable to pollution than their inshore cousins, already adapted to the chemical hassle of coastal waters. Witness the current pressure to dump further and further away from shore. If the prediction is correct, such dumping is not (or should not be, if anyone pays attention to plankton) a viable option.

As it turns out, dumping anywhere may reduce plankton and thus the ocean's productivity.

In the North Sea, persistent industrial pollutants may have caused a dramatic decline of larger ocean phytoplankton. The state of ocean science is tantalizingly sparse in this regard. Larger plankton out in the ocean may have just as well declined merely for natural reasons. Here at home, scientists watched while a barge with the untoward name *Sparkling Water* dumped a million liters of American Cyanamid chemical waste into the 106-mile offshore

New York Bight dump site, one of two U.S. deepwater ocean dumps for industrial waste. Plankton size diminished; productivity deteriorated. Woods Hole investigators compared the growth of plankton clones, one from the coast, the other from the ocean, in the same polluted solution. The ocean clone was "invariably more sensitive to chemical stress." Until now, ocean plankton have had no need to protect themselves, accustomed as they are to a stable environment. "They have thin skins," one scientist says.

Plankton apparently cannot coexist with pollution. But plankton are the basis of ocean production. "Without these microscopic plants all ocean life from the smallest shrimp to the largest whale would perish. . . . If too many [plankton] die, the oxygen content of the atmosphere will fall and earth will become another dead planet." This dictum, which nobody believes very likely, comes from the U.S. Department of Interior, the very department that licenses citizens to dump in the ocean, thus bringing the dread happening closer.

The pollution threat to plankton takes place in the microscopic world we do not see. Not so the fish kill, a very visible danger signal from the sea. Thousands of fish may suddenly turn belly up in the water or cover beaches with a tangled, odiferous decaying mass. Within hours the event is headline news. Unexpected, it shocks and scares.

Suffocation by anoxia—lack of oxygen—is a common cause. To "breathe," the fish opens its mouth, brings water in, then forces water out over its thin-walled filamented gills, bright red with capillaries that lace their surface. Here the vital exchange—carbon dioxide for oxygen—takes place fast and efficiently. Seventy-five percent of the oxygen in a gulp of seawater goes into the fish's blood for its body cells, joining with oxygen absorbed through the skin.

Toss a captured fish into the bottom of a boat and its gills expand to their limit, reaching for oxygen, then the fish collapses, unable to exist out of its water world. It is not much better off in water clouded with sediment from garbage or sewage that has been dumped offshore. Sediment clogs gills, impedes respiration, often permanently affecting gill surfaces, just as dirty air affects our lungs. If there is not enough oxygen in the water, the fish suffocates and dies. So does all marine life in the neighborhood.

There are very occasional oxygen failures from natural causes. Several were recorded in the nineteenth century, half a dozen in the early twentieth century. Man-made mass mortalities are frequent modern phenomena. Nutrients from sewage and agricultural runoff cause major blooms of phytoplankton in the sea, sometimes enough to change the color of the water. When these blooms die back, the oxygen supply is used up, causing mass mortalities of fish and other bottom life. In the 1970s, low levels of dissolved oxygen killed 45,000 fish off Florida; in Mobile Bay on the Gulf of Mexico, oxygen depletion sometimes traps disoriented dying fish close enough to shore to be netted by people who live there. They call such an event "a jubilee."

These macabre fishing celebrations are now only too common. Anoxia occurs when the ocean is glutted with more organic matter than it can handle. Normally, ocean residents which die before they are eaten, sink to the bottom where bacteria decompose them into their elements, using oxygen in the process. Nothing is wasted. The elements resurface, are again transformed by the sun, completing the cycle. Add sewage and you get an over-rich surface, more work for bacteria, and greatly multiplied demands for oxygen. Several thousand times more nutrients show up, even in treated sewage, than those naturally in seawater.

When there is too much organic material, the demand for oxygen exceeds the supply. The cycle is disrupted, the water becomes anoxic, and the jubilee begins.

A massive kill off the mid-Atlantic states in 1976 was "an environmental event of epic proportions," says Carl Sindermann, director of the National Marine Fisheries Service Laboratory at Sandy Hook, New Jersey. Sindermann's studies have made this one of the best-analyzed fish kills in history. Shellfish and fish were killed

49

by the thousands, starting in July, continuing through October. Some 147,000 metric tons of surf clams were destroyed along with ocean quahogs and sea scallops; Lobster catches were reduced by half. Cruises to assess the damage had to be extended further and further south, Sindermann says, and many kilometers seaward. Oxygen-deficient bottom water, sometimes with zero oxygen levels, carpeted a huge lifeless corridor in the sea.

For years, waste from the coast streamed into these waters. When millions more people moved in, the volume multiplied. When would the waste overfertilize the sea, causing the marine lifeline to fail? Even the smartest computer could not figure that out, given the natural and unnatural variables that had to be taken into account. The computer could only predict inevitable disaster.

In 1976 the moment arrived. There happened to be an unusual combination of abnormal south winds, high spring temperatures, early warming of surface water, a massive phytoplankton bloom. This mix demanded more oxygen than expected, which, along with huge demands from man-made waste, caused the catastrophe. Oxygen levels have sagged badly ever since. "The entire sector is very marginal," Sindermann says. "It may be pushed over the edge into anoxia in any year. . . ."

For all time the ocean system has provided oxygen to its inhabitants. The burden of late-twentieth-century wastes occasionally overwhelms this ability. There are limits to what the ocean can handle and still keep functioning. There is not enough oxygen to take care of both the bacteria at work on disintegrating so much waste and the fish in the sea. The price of such ocean use is the fish kill.

This is the base of the new self-destruct pyramid. The next level, many times more sophisticated, sickens fish and threatens our lives somewhat more directly.

Some wastes that are washed or dumped into the ocean do not need bacteria; nor do they deplete the water's oxygen supply. Instead, waste ingredients such as heavy metals, toxic chemicals, synthetic hydrocarbons do not distingrate or decompose only slowly and are too often accumulated in fish flesh and the tissues of other marine life, posing a threat as man eats fish.

More minerals are now put in the sea than have ever accosted marine life before. In the matter of simple metals, for example, natural geological processes send 25 million metric tons of iron cascading into the ocean; we add 319 million metric tons. Natural copper in the ocean is 375,000 metric tons; we add 4½ million— and so down the metal roster to antimony, which we multiply forty times.

These new amounts make a savage difference. One of the first carefully recorded results was in the small coastal town of Minamata, Japan, where, starting in 1953, cats went mad and died and citizens suffered severe neurological disease ending, for many, in death, for others in permanent grotesque disabilities.

The source of the trouble was a mystery. After long investigation, it was found that both cats and people were suffering from mercury poisoning, because of the fish they ate. Enough deadly mercury had built up in fish flesh to cause those who ate it symptoms of penetration of the central nervous system and the brain. "When the symptoms begin . . . it is much too late to do anything to reverse the course of poisoning," Anthony Tucker says in a graphic description of the event. "Anyone who eats one normal meal of fish contaminated by organic mercury to levels between 5 parts per million (ppm) and 15 ppm every day will most certainly be disabled and will probably die."

It took years to pinpoint where the poison came from. A manufacturing plant on the shores of Minamata Bay was a suspect, but the mercury it discharged with its wastes into the water was inorganic, relatively safe in modest quantities. The mercury in fish and shellfish in the bay was the deadly organic form—dimethyl mercury—and that was not produced by the factory.

Only man's chemistry could transform one into the other, or so it was believed. In 1967, fourteen years after the poisoning started,

Swedish scientists discovered that the transformation can occur in the sea with no help from man, perhaps by microbes' action when oxygen levels are low.

What the fish and shellfish of Minamata had eaten and stored in their flesh was created by nature's alchemy. Possibly the sea has always acted on inorganic mercury this way. Perhaps there never was enough of it in one place before to be noticed. Countless chemical reactions are taking place to substances we put into the big lake, and some have been discovered, enough to support the generalization that almost nothing is impervious to the sea and that such sea actions are unlikely to be benign. We are at the beginning of finding out.

The poisoning at Minamata and the suffocation of marine life off New Jersey were obvious. The mass kill is visible, identifiable, with at least a hope of being prevented in the future. In contrast is the emerging worry over less obvious sublethal happenings.

Sublethal doesn't quite kill but it causes harm, sometimes enough harm to bring about death. We are reluctant to accept the harming concept; it is somehow more difficult than facing death itself. Striped bass, for example, caused consternation when 200 to 400 large stripers inexplicably perished in Long Island Sound a year or two ago. The threat of danger was erased with the discovery that a certain localized bacteria in the water had killed the fish. Only recently, as their diminution has been noticed, do we admit to concern about what is happening to the stripers which survive.

Scientists agree that problems which develop from sublethal effects demand our attention, now, before it is too late. Something sublethal is happening to striped bass which is causing what the U.S. Fish and Wildlife Service calls a "mysterious decline." In Chesapeake Bay, where the fish are most abundant, 30.4 young stripers per haul showed up in 1970, 1.9 in 1980, and 1.2 in 1981. Nineteen eighty-two was the poorest baby bass crop in twenty-eight years. In New York State, a 24-inch minimum was put in force in

1983 to give existing bass a chance to grow to spawning age. Nevertheless, the species seems to hurtle toward extinction.

Most of these fish spend their first years in the Chesapeake before migrating to cooler North Atlantic waters. A smaller number are born and grow up in New York's Hudson River. Both river and bay are loaded with polychlorinated biphenyl (PCB), the man-made compound which was dumped there in the 1970s. Like DDT, PCBs break down only slowly in water and seem prepared to stay in the biosphere for at least several decades.

When PCBs meet bass eggs and larvae, eggs fail to hatch, hatchlings fail to live. The conspicuous decline of the species is now thought by some scientists to be due to the sublethal effect of PCB on young bass. It maims and deforms them; backbones weakened, they cannot grow properly, find food, or summon the energy to migrate and reproduce.

PCB is highly soluble in fat. When eaten by bass, or taken up from the water through gills, it slips through the fish's intestinal wall to lodge in fatty tissues where it accumulates, a process discovered only in 1976. The longer the fish lives, the more PCB it ingests. A rock bass collected in the Hudson River registered a PCB level of 350 ppm, the highest concentration ever found, seventy times more than the official, safe level. Scientists say the actual level is 2 ppm or 1 ppm. "We'll get this on the books when we get a new president," one of them comments.

If a bass escapes being killed or maimed by PCB, the toxic collected in its flesh will pass along to its predator, most likely an enthusiastic fisherman who consideres himself lucky to have landed the delectable, increasingly rare striper. A bass banquet could deliver damage to the diner's liver, nervous system, cause skin lesions, possibly birth defects, possibly cancer. Because PCB is fat-soluble, it lodges easily in women's breasts where it combines with mother's milk.

Two General Electric plants on the Hudson released between

2 and 30 pounds of PCBs into the river every day. The waters coursing to the sea had far more than the five parts per million (ppm) considered legally safe by the federal government for human consumption. Even so, it took the state and the EPA six years to finally stop GE's dumping, by which time 640,000 pounds of PCBs were lacing Hudson water used by some 150,000 residents. Dredging the river to remove at least some of it has long been planned, will cost hundreds of millions of dollars, take ten years at least, and destroy the Hudson's bottom life.

In December, 1982, the state of New Jersey banned the sale of striped bass caught in four river basins and advised residents to restrict their eating of the bass and four other fish to once a week. Basis of the warning is a six-year study of cancer-causing PCB contamination in these fish. Neighboring New York State, too, warned against eating striped bass from the Hudson. And in New Bedford, Massachusetts, later discussed in detail, 1,000 times more PCB than in any other place in the nation contaminates the harbor. Fishing there has been stopped, and citizens are uneasy, alarmed about what has been described as their underwater Love Canal.

George Woodwell, distinguished scientist at Woods Hole, believes that by now, every living creature has some PCB in its body, or soon will have. "The problem needs immediate attention," he says. So do pollutants such as the deadly Kepone, washing out to sea from the James River in Virginia and elsewhere, and radioactive waste, the waste beyond comprehension, still at a relatively low level.

Master polluter of them all is oil. No more facile a murderer is at large in the ocean at this writing. Released by man's ingenuity, from its rock tombs under the sea, oil's sublethal effects can devastate. Like garbage and sewage it suffocates, like the mercury at Minamata it poisons. Like PCB it maims and deforms the young of the species; like many pollutants it may eliminate larger plankton in favor of smaller plankton. It contains deadly carcinogens. It is toxic to fish eggs and larvae, the hope of the future of their kind.

Oil is at once the same as many ocean pollutants but unique among them. It is the most prevalent pollutant in the ocean. The National Academy of Science in 1975 put the amount of oil entering the ocean at 6.1 million tons per year, over a billion dollars worth. In 1982, the United Nations published the same figure as the "best recent estimate." The American Petroleum Institute is preparing a new, much lower figure to reflect what it claims are safer oil operations, but independent analyses point to increasing amounts. Oil is not only more in amount than any other pollutant, but also in geographical spread, being added to the ocean all over the world.

These are years of petrorevelation. We know more about oil at large in the sea than ever before. Understanding the oil threat to marine life deepens.

"That oil is toxic is now beyond dispute." Years of study and the research of many peers made it possible finally for Dr. Robert Howarth of the Ecosystems Center, Marine Biological Laboratory at Woods Hole, Massachusetts, to write that sentence in 1983. Oil is toxic at concentrations well below 10 ppb, Howarth says. By contrast, an oil spill can douse marine life with concentrations as great as 7,000 times this, an event which staggers the imagination.

The first terrible days of an oil spill attest to oil's toxicity. Death is immediate. The blackened stinking blankets of bodies on the beach or rocky shore is the visible result. An unforgettable example is the breakup of the tanker *Amoco Cadiz* off Brittany in 1978, spilling a quarter of a million tons of oil into the sea. On its way ashore the oil lapped a rocky bird sanctuary, killing 3,000 seabirds. "Sea urchins washed up on beaches in windrows, 16 million per mile of beach," an observer reports. "Later came the razor clams, then cockles . . . a 2,000 acre salt marsh 90 miles [away] was covered waist-deep in oil." Oil covered oyster beds, killed finfish. Residents painted signs, *"La mer est morte."*

Oil killed the entire crop of local seaweed that supplied 75 percent of France, destroyed the fishing business and 80 percent of

the oyster crop. Marine biologists estimate a seven- to ten-year recovery time for the badly battered Brittany coast. The estimate may
be low for parts of this coast. Residence time for oil, deep in beach
sands and underwater sediments, has only recently become known.
Howarth and a Woods Hole colleague, John Teal, compiled many
scientists' data on recent, large, well-known spills, giving us new
hard-edge facts. Oil, they say, stays in sediments for at least twelve
years, which is as long as the record has been kept to date. Best
guess for oil spilled in the Straits of Magellan in 1974 is fifteen to
thirty years on the beaches, over a hundred years for sheltered tidal
flats and marshes.

Oil is a mix, hundreds of hydrocarbons welded together over
the millennia. Lighter than water, spilled oil forms a slick that slides
across the sea, killing whatever might swim across its path, terrifying coast dwellers. When the slick starts to "weather" and break
up, there is general relief. People assume the threat is over, the oil
gone. As it turns out, the reverse is true.

The oil exists, unseen, a portion of it more virulent than before, having become more toxic, carcinogenic and water-soluble
while floating in the sun. It has oxidized, adding oxygen atoms to
its hydrocarbons. The transformation has been a secret for so long,
Howarth tells us, because studies took place under artificial light
in the laboratory where the change could not happen.

New facts deny us the sigh of relief. When the oil slick disappears, it is, instead, time to worry. Some of the altered oil sinks
to the sea floor, where it is by no means less troublesome. It is
transported there in fecal pellets of zooplankton, innocently grazing in the slick. One investigator says a typical zooplankton population could transport a remarkable 3 tons of oil per square kilo-
meter to the bottom every day. Another route is hitching a ride on
sediment particles swirling in the water. Adding an oil droplet makes
enough weight for a swift trip to the bottom, be it miles down in
the deep or in the shallows near shore.

Oil kills on the bottom as on the beach. The population perishes or escapes, if it can crawl or swim away. Species which can survive such an oil bath move in. Like other opportunistic species, they are of a lower, tougher evolutionary order than the regular residents, less productive, less diverse. The oil sinks into the sediments where, as noted, it is likely to stay. Opportunists take over, moving evolution down a step, and the resident oil, oozing out of the sediments for years, keeps it that way.

Oil in the big lake is an all-around blue ribbon pollutant. It destroys plankton, fish eggs, larvae, sensitive marine organisms. Its carcinogenic hydrocarbons are incorporated into human food sources. It is toxic when spilled into the sea and may get more so. It can stay in the sediments for at least twelve years, perhaps for a century. We manage to put a billion dollars a year worth of this molten gold into the ocean where it becomes poison dross. How we do it and how we deal with its effects constitute a contemporary Gothic tale that requires a chapter of its own.

5
OIL ON
THE LOOSE

The present frenzied search for oil under the seabed has an intensity that borders on insanity. Oil must be found, the consequences of the search be damned. The Outer Continental Shelf (OCS), which edges the continent, seems the most likely place to find more oil, and it is there that modern man's remarkable machines drill down into the rock in the ocean deep, crazed giant dentists urged onward by a fearful society.

Fear is born of the idea that oil is indispensable—"the indispensable motive fuel of a modern state," Walter Levy, international oil expert says—and that the amount of it buried in the globe is almost gone. Early in the twenty-first century—estimates differ on the exact time—there will be no more oil. Its span on the globe is "two billion B.C.–A.D. two thousand" a British oil analyst says, and a voluminous M.I.T. study agrees: "The time when oil will plateau and then decline is clearly in sight."

Oil might run out before the frenzied search for it wrecks too many people's existence. How much oil is left? There is no one supportable figure. Expert estimators from the U.S. Geological Survey to the American Petroleum Institute and many in between come up with varying amounts. There could be oil so deeply buried that the cost of retrieval would be prohibitive, even to oil companies. The amount depends on guesses of what's available in the USSR and China, on possibilities known as "undiscovered recoverable amounts," and on who is doing the guessing.

Adding all these apples and oranges, the total remaining oil on the globe is said to be somewhere between 569 billion barrels and 670.7 billion barrels. In the U.S., the Department of Energy says there are 29.8 billion barrels left, the Department of Interior says 58 billion barrels, other estimates fall in between, with more recent estimates being lower. The world used some 23 billion barrels in 1981, of which the U.S. had a lion's share, more than 6 billion barrels. An optimistic scenario gives us a maximum five decades of world use at the present rate. Of this, U.S. offshore oil might provide a modest 2 to 5 percent.

To lose the indispensable fuel is of such extreme concern that people reject the certainty out of hand, seize on every oil discovery as a reprieve. Stepped-up technology allowed increased probes of the OCS in the last decade; by the early '80s, a quarter of the world's oil came from under the sea. Of necessity, this has turned a goodly amount of oil loose in the ocean. On the loose, oil is a danger to the future of fish, shellfish, marine mammals, and man. The harder we search for OCS oil, the worse the danger becomes. There is no way to search and find without spilling oil into the sea, although industry can do much better than it often does. Lacking is respect for the ocean.

Oil in a container has long been an everyday comfort. One kind of oil or another—olive, whale—lit the graceful terra cotta lamps of the ancient Greeks, provided the flickering flames of brass and glass lamps in nineteenth-century parlors. Oil from the earth—petroleum—is secure in the car tank, the furnace tank, the cluster of great round storage tanks on the outskirts of town. Now oil escapes containment. Roaming at large in the ocean, it transforms from a comfortable commodity to a terrifying antagonist, a peril to life. The short-term goal of collecting what is left collides with long-term protection of the ocean environment.

Soon, energy must be found elsewhere. The complexities of discovering alternatives is not part of the ocean story. What is important here is that the present focus on oil is loading the ocean with millions of gallons of petroleum hydrocarbons. In 1982, with staggering disregard for the newly discovered effects of oil in the ocean on people and fish, and the futility of chasing the last oil drops, the Reagan administration put a billion OCS acres up for lease sale in the ensuing five years, nearly the entire OCS of the United States.

Former U.S. Secretary of the Interior Watt staged the super-sale, tossing in fishing grounds well known for their astounding productivity, sensitive coast areas, and fragile ecosystems. The Environmental Protection Agency (EPA), which might have prevented this move, had become a political toy, reduced in size, corrupted to unreliability. The new OCS proposal had to be challenged by the states together with environmental organizations, privately financed, and is at this date before the courts.

Most people believe that oil is loose in the ocean by accident. An approximate ten percent seeps from the earth, a natural phenomenon. The rest is no accident. It is there because we put it there, somewhere between 3 and 7 million tons of it, added each year, floating loose. This huge amount is what it costs to maneuver undersea oil, and oil from across the sea, into the containers of our high-energy society. We put it in the ocean by oil spills, oil well blowouts, oil tankers breaking up at sea, or simply by washing out the crankcase of a car. We let oil run off city streets into the sea or pour down from the atmosphere where it has been sent by noxious fumes.

Watch the headlines or TV news. A tanker breakup is billed as an accident, an oil well blowout is an accident, a broken underwater oil pipeline is an accident. A recent book on pollution includes a section on intentional pollution (dumping in Long Island Sound), another on accidental pollution (the breakup of oil tanker *Amoco Cadiz*). There is no difference between them. The number of dumpers is known; the number of oil spills to expect each year (at least one over 25,000 tons) is known. And we put tankers to sea, well informed on the percentage that will founder or otherwise meet their demise. The only surprise, the only accident, is when, where, and how much, and even these facts are now computerized in most of their dimensions.

If oil let loose in the sea is considered an accident, then it is nobody's fault, nobody's responsibility. Thus pollution is comfortably beyond reason. Its effects, believed inevitable, are simply an earth tax which the nation, having applied a few well-placed Band-Aids, appears willing to pay. Actually it is a conscious, informed decision, a choice made by the body politic, believing the ocean can take it, indeed must take it for the sake of oil.

We pay this tax with poisoned shellfish, disappearing fish population, damaged shore birds and seabirds, with blackened beaches and oil-bearing sediments on the bottom of the coastal seas.

Now the U.S. proposes to pay with a venerable life pattern that has been hacked out of the wilderness over thousands of years, the rare endemic culture of natives who live in villages around Norton Sound, off the Bering Sea, Alaska, near the USSR border. Their forefathers trekked across the land bridge that once spanned the sea, connecting Asia and America. Some new arrivals went south, some stayed to settle in the snow and ice. Their descendants, known as Eskimos or Native Americans, still subsist on the wildlife of this place. That is their life.

The great Yukon River, fourth largest in America, empties its riches into Norton Sound and the northern Bering Sea. Its nutrients attract swarms of birds, fish, all manner of seals, walrus, whales. More than a million ringed seals, 15,000 or more gray whales, 80 percent of the world population of walrus moves through the area. So do most of the continent's whistling swans, the greatest concentration of geese in North America, the highest densities of all waterfowl, a western variety of salmon which swarms out of the Yukon to carry out the same life cycle as their eastern relatives.

The crowds of wildlife enjoying the fruits of the Yukon provide, in turn, for the people who live around this Alaskan cove. Their life continues old traditions, fishing, hunting, berrying, building small villages convenient to the walrus route, or to seal, salmon, or whale. They eat what they catch, carve the ivory, sew the skins or trade the take with other villages.

The Sound now attracts new kinds of hunters, oil hunters who believe there could be oil under these freezing waters. Never explored for oil before, Norton Sound—Lease Sale No. 57—holds the bold title Frontier Area, and excites the even bolder desire to dig there. The U.S. Geological Survey's informed guess is that 480 million barrels of oil and considerable amounts of gas are there under the sea floor. There is a 14 percent chance of finding it. If found and recovered, it would keep the U.S. in oil for less than one month. Extracting and shipping the oil would forever change Alaskan village life and its wildlife support system.

"The issue is survival," a villager says. "Survival for the majority civilization is contingent on energy. Survival for the coastal Eskimos is contingent on the sea, the land, and its ability to provide for life." Here in the long blue-lavender ice shadows, men struggle to dominate the freezing fertile waters for their own separate purposes.

This is the first time in the U.S.A., to my knowledge, that the push for oil directly and consciously attacks man, for whose benefit it presumably is undertaken. In pamphlets, Norton Sound villagers vociferously oppose Lease Sale No. 57 in language that shows the strength of people who know what they are talking about. They testify to days on end in their land when snow falls so thickly that you cannot see 10 feet and could not possibly work on an oil spill. They describe the impact of ice jams, moving fast, of the strong onshore afternoon winds that would carry oil onto the land, the severe geohazards that would prevent oil cleanup. They describe the wildlife habitat, the needs of its occupants.

In the opposite corner is the 5-pound, 500-page Norton Sound Environmental Impact Statement (EIS) prepared by the U.S. Interior Department under the aegis of Secretary Watt. Required for the sale, it is encyclopedic rather than analytic. Figures on projected oil spills are based on Gulf of Mexico experience, irrelevant considering the difference in climate. Possibilities for prevention, cleanup, and impact on Norton Sound are guesswork.

If the lease-sale goes through, the balance between villagers and wildlife will change. Old values will shift to oil values. The oil boom, if there is one, will affect shoreline citizens as it has done elsewhere, abroad. I remember a gently curving beach in Borneo from which I gazed, disbelieving, at the line of oil rigs in the placid aquamarine water, and at the residents of the town, now distinctly part of the oil culture. I remember the recent transformation of Stävanger, a thousand-year-old Norwegian fishing village, into a booming port for North Sea oil.

Norton Sound villagers vigorously reject this future. They value and want to prevent the lifestyle that has lasted for thousands of years, killing only for subsistence. They know that oil loose in their waters will endanger the wildlife, basis of their existence.

We are prepared to smash this ancient American culture for a possible few weeks' supply of oil. In January 1983, Alaska's Governor Sheffield and Secretary Watt made a deal. "I am pleased to announce . . ." Watt promised, "protection of the valued subsistence lifestyle of coastal communities and of sensitive environmental resources," a promise so at odds with the lease-sale as to be meaningless. For extras, he extended the lease to ten years from the usual five, to "give time to study the impacts." The extension acts as a dead hand, prolonging Watt's judgment after his departure from Interior. Cancelation of such leases, should a new administration so desire, is possible but unlikely, due to the tremendous expense involved.

Immediately following the deal, Governor Sheffield went to a series of fund-raising events in New York, Houston, Dallas, and Denver that were attended by oil executives. He raised enough to repay himself for campaign expenses. Alaska State Senator Frank Ferguson sued Sheffield and two aides for violation of the state's conflict-of-interest law.

There are other Norton Sounds. Many Eskimo communities along Alaska's north coast stand to be affected by Watt's leasing program. "We are on the verge of a mammoth effort to exploit Alaskan [oil] resources," Melville Conant, Exxon oil consultant, says. Twenty billion dollars have already been invested for Alaskan OCS oil; the total may run to $300 billion if demand for oil continues. If we can destroy one culture for oil, we will destroy others. Next it may be your life, or mine.

The long view lays a new perspective on the short view, the present passion for oil. Science has deciphered the very beginnings of oil and its peregrinations through the earth. Its time on the globe is something of a remarkable romance.

In a triumph of recycling, the ocean made oil from the remains of life. Billions of little corpses of marine life forms, mostly the familiar plankton, plus animal and vegetable debris, were the raw materials. The transformation to the combustible black fluid required several million years, and some spectacular rock shifts. The timing was quite precise. It awaited the collection of enough raw materials on the bottom of the sea, and an era when the ocean had invaded the land sufficiently deeply to form basins where these sediments could collect.

During Cretaceous times, 136 to 65 million years ago, an unexplained vast explosion in numbers of marine organisms appeared in the sea. At some time between this sudden superpopulation and the Paleocene era, 65 to 54 million years ago, the moment of oil creation arrived. Enough little corpses had collected in the sedimentary basins. They were acted on by bacteria and by the heat of tectonic processes, were compressed under rock where they would undergo chemical change over several million years. The result—oil and gas.

These accumulated in porous rock, were moved around by continental drift, folded into rock fissures, hidden at last in the chambers of impermeable rock. The largest discoveries—the Middle East fields, Alaska's Beaufort Sea—are in Cretaceous sediments, neatly supporting the scientific timetable. Only recently, by global time, has this mix of thousands of chemicals, mostly hydrocarbons, formed by the sea's slow-acting chemistry, been discovered and, in this era, almost exhausted.

In less than a century we have invented ways to uncork oil under the sea from its ocean tombs. The first U.S. offshore oil well was drilled from a wooden platform in California shallows in 1894. Now there are 26,000 wells off U.S. coasts, and oilmen are intent on advancing technology to reach the final gallons wherever they may be hidden under the waves. A 1982 record was set off France with a well drilled in almost a mile of water in the Mediterranean, a considerable feat. Other engineering wonders are enormous drilling and living platforms on legs, semisubmersible barges, and production systems totally submerged on the sea floor. With an eye to the Arctic, a new design on the drawing boards is the colossal drill platform supported by a single concrete column to break up the ice.

The first effort in history to crack the Outer Continental Shelf of the Atlantic Coast was made in 1979 by the drill ship *Glomar Pacific*, chartered by Exxon for this historic occasion. The oil company spent a year and a million dollars to prepare the ship for its lead position and for stormy East Coast weather. When I visited the ship during the first days of its historic assignment, it was trim, taut, and dazzling as a champion racehorse ready for the big day. It rode at anchor off Atlantic City, its bright blue winch covers, scarlet cab towering over white cranes, brilliant yellow traveling block, combined to provide a festive air.

For Exxon and others that were to drill in the Baltimore Canyon, this was serious business. It was a big investment. Nine companies spent $1.75 billion gambling that the mid-Atlantic OCS, virgin territory, would yield recoverable amounts of oil and gas. (It didn't.) The oilmen risked more than money. Tampering with the crust of the earth, particularly that part of it that lies under the sea, carries a powerful potential for violence. There is considerable danger

68

to the eighty-man crew who work under such pressure that they need two weeks off after two weeks of work on the rig.

To ward off trouble, all kinds of safety devices crowd the ship. The drill, cutting its way twenty-four hours a day into undersea rock, is under constant surveillance, monitored by a battery of computers, a TV camera on the ocean floor, an automatic positioner which holds the huge ship within inches of the single crucial drilling spot.

But even the best modern technology does not prevent fearsome blowouts, one way that oil slips free into the ocean. With the 1983 U.S. state-of-the-art, we can expect one blowout for every 250 OCS wells, the U.S. Geological Survey says. The rate for blowouts around the world may be much higher. Best known in the U.S. is the 1969 Santa Barbara blowout which poured forth 2 million gallons of oil. The terrifying sight was viewed by millions on TV. Robert Eastman's *Black Tide*, an early account, belives it set off the environmental era of the '70s, helped along, ironically, by California's then-Governor Reagan, who has since become one of the nation's most potent environment wreckers.

In 1977, the Ekofisk well in the icy North Sea blew out, catapulting thousands of gallons of crude oil into the tempestuous waters. Two years later, across the ocean, the worst oil spill ever, at this writing, was the Ixtoc blowout in Campeche Bay, Mexico, where 140 million gallons, twice as much as from any other oil catastrophe, poured into the Gulf. For ten months, experts brought from all over the world could not cap the well. The oil sank, evaporated in the atmosphere, or floated in great dark masses across the Gulf, heading for the Texas coast.

Oil spills or blowouts usually have an immediate impact, with a day or two leeway at most before oil hits the shore. This spill was different, ideal for investigation, as there were weeks in which to get ready while the oil traversed the Gulf. The U.S. ad hoc Response Team, headed by the Coast Guard and including 200 scientists from government, universities, and private institutions,

69

assembled in Corpus Christi. Helicopters charted movement of the approaching oil mass. The press swarmed around officialdom, waiting for impact. Before-and-after measurements were planned to collect pristine information on the effects weathered oil would have.

It was a tantalizing circumstance.

And an opportunity missed. Most of the money promised to the National Oceanic and Atmospheric Administration (NOAA) for the investigation never materialized. Most measurements of what happened to weathered oil, to beach creatures, to offshore sediments and beach sands were not made, and people will not find out for some years whether eating shrimps from the coast has given them cancer.

The state-of-the-art of cleaning up spilled oil did emerge from the *Ixtoc* disaster. The Response Team helped Mexicans at the blowout site. They used skimmers and dispersants, in 10- to 12-foot seas with 40-knot winds. They cleaned up 5,000 barrels a day, "a drop in the bucket," Coast Guard Captain Charles Corbett, co-chairman of the Team, says. Most of the 140 million gallons moved across the Gulf, skirting or sinking under the Texas coast defenses that had been set up to trap the oil. Oil lay in great foul black tarmats, a hitherto unknown formation, on the beach, in the marshes, and wallowed just offshore, rising heavily with the waves.

Cleanup crews removing the semisolid oil had frequent attacks of headaches, nausea, and vomiting so that the operation had to be slowed and pregnant women and children barred from the scene. There were signs that oil had become more toxic than ever in its weeks of floating in the sun and sea. Corbett's view is that very little can be done to clean up massive blowouts in remote spots. An assistant put it more bluntly: "If you try to work against nature," he told me, "you end up with your butt in a slick."

The hard sell of oil companies that a blowout is an accident allows us to believe it might not happen again. The facts show it to be a built-in cost of retrieving OCS oil. In the Persian Gulf in

1983, it became a weapon. Two Iranian wells, bombed by Iraq, gushed 2,000 barrels a day into the Gulf. There were disastrous consequences to desalinization plants which supplied six Gulf Arab nations with water, there being few natural water sources in their lands. The Arabs bought out bottled water supplies, prayed in mosques for mercy, and complained that their fish tasted like tar. Their fresh-water supply dwindled.

Eight months later, more than 10,000 barrels of crude gushed daily from nine wells. Oil spill expert Red Adair says, "It is probably the worst thing I've ever seen." It is difficult to get accurate information, Walter Levy, international oil expert, says. However, he believes that the situation "appears to have been under control since late in 1983."

Oil spills are a frequent cost. "This is the Age of Oil Spills," the *New York Times* announces. "We have 10,000 spills a year. . . ." The U.S. Geological Survey says a single platform will have at least one, possibly three, major spills, 1,000 barrels or more, in its twenty-year life. It will have some twenty-five medium spills, and 2,000 little spills of less than 50 barrels. These numbers, shocking as they are, come from years of digging wells in the Gulf and off southern California in shallow, calm water. They are freely used by proponents of digging in the stormy North Atlantic and frozen Arctic OCS to predict what is likely to happen, although, clearly, the statistics could have little meaning in the untried circumstances of the Frontier—the cold, rough, windy northern waters. More to the point is the experience of the British coastline on the North Sea: Scotland, the Orkneys, and the Shetland Islands. In 1973, at the start of the digging, there were twenty-five oil spills; in 1978 over 100; in 1980 over 200.

Dug out of the ocean, oil has to be moved to where it is needed, another source of spills. The more oil moved, the more spilled. In 1980 it was seven times what it had been seven years earlier.

Oil is mostly moved by tankers. Despite regulations, tankers

71

put oil in the sea by cleaning ballast tanks and pumping bilge. They collide, crash into rocks, break apart in storms. The major tanker tragedies are developing a litany—*Torrey Canyon*, 1967, 700,000 barrels; *Argo Merchant*, 1976, 7.5 million barrels; *Amoco Cadiz*, 1978, 1.5 million barrels (and more than a billion dollars worth of claims arising from it) . . . and so it continues. There are about 7,000 oil tankers in the world. U.S. tankers are elderly; the *Argo Merchant*, known in the trade as "the old rust bucket," and the rest of the fleet averaged eleven years of age in 1982. Most tankers are registered in Liberia to avoid safety regulations. They average seven years of age, but only the youngest are required to meet Coast Guard dictates for improved steering equipment and protective ballast location.

Everywhere a portion of the oil we capture from under the sea escapes. Even huge, brand-new LOOP, the nation's first superport, built off the Louisiana coast at the cost of $770 million, admits to frequent small spills. They come from a totally unanticipated error, a tiny detail in the floating supership port. The hose that connects a tanker to LOOP has gaskets that wear out, allowing oil to decamp into the water.

Before offshore oil was discovered, no one paid much attention to who owned the continental margin. These public lands were freely used for fishing, swimming, shipping. When California started leasing seabed lots to oil companies for healthy profits, the nation claimed its underwater acreage in the name of all the people. President Roosevelt and his secretary of the interior, Harold Ickes, started the move, and President Truman used his presidential prerogatives to proclaim the OCS U.S. property. Congress then passed a law, the OCS Lands Act, which put the secretary of interior in charge.

Undersea real estate was offered for lease-sale to oil companies for development. The price was huge, the income enormous, for landlord and tenant alike. It is, in fact, the second largest single source of federal income after taxes. Complications came in the 1970s when the effects of oil on marine life started to be understood, just as the government greatly accelerated leasing. Environmentalists pushed for survival rights of fish and fishermen, states pushed for coastal control, and oil companies opposed any change that would limit golden undersea opportunities. It took most of the 1970s to amend the law, giving the states more autonomy and the environment more protection. The measure finally passed in 1977.

At this moment the virgin East Coast OCS was put up for lease. First was the Baltimore Canyon, where the *Glomar Pacific*'s bright colors rolled on the waves and no one found any oil. Next on the block—an incredible stretch of the North Atlantic, Georges Bank, known to be one of the most prolific fishing grounds in the world. In the early '70s, catches per unit area were twice those of the North Sea, four times those of the famed Canadian Grand Banks, Richard Hennemuth, director of the NMFS laboratory in Woods Hole, says. This small stretch of shallow water, some 100 to 300 miles off Cape Cod, is a natural national treasure.

It is marvelously ingenious in its arrangement. Only 10 to 15 feet deep in its shallowest places, sunshine can penetrate its lower regions, enriching bottom water. The Bank is exceedingly turbulent, constantly mixing this nutritious broth into its system, creating an excellent environment for fish eggs and larvae which float on the surface. The circling gyre current keeps the water swirling around the Bank, and gently perambulates the early floating stages of fish. The 200 or more species that spawn at Georges are mostly offshore floaters in contrast to Gulf fish; their early stages largely grow in the marshes. (The oil companies, Howarth tells us, are "making a mess of those marshes, truly a horror story!") Georges Bank fish are 90 percent edible, as against Gulf fish, most of which are used for agricultural purposes.

Some, like cod, haddock, and yellowtail, spend their lives on the Bank. It is a spectacular fishing ground. Others migrate. Georges alumni account for almost three quarters of the catch from Maine to North Carolina and, wherever they may be, add up to 1.8 billion pounds of fish per year.

At the leasing of Georges—Lease Sale No. 42—the battle was joined. The conflict being best use of the area known to be a superb fish habitat and thought to be a source of oil. The Conservation Law Foundation in Boston and other environmental organizations believed coexistence was impossible, given the present irreverence for the sea by government and oil companies. Chronic oil spills over Georges would put oil in the water. Trapped by the gyre along with the fish, oil would attach to fish eggs, sink to the bottom to poison the fish's diet. Ten parts per billion can cause a 40 percent mortality in plaice eggs, 20 parts per billion can reduce phytoplankton to smaller species, which, as has been said, may eventually reduce the size of predators. Because Georges Bank is a miracle of fertility, it is particularly vulnerable. The possibilities of disaster are known but more time and money for research are needed for hard-edged facts. They are slow in coming. "The capacity to drag feet in discovering the effects of oil in water is infinite," Howard Sanders, Woods Hole scientist, says.

Through 1977, '78, and most of '79, the fight over use of Georges Bank continued on successive levels of the judicial system. "If there ever was a public interest case, this is it," one of its judges said. Interest ran high. Eventually, the oil companies and the Department of Interior had their way, the sale took place and rigs invaded the fish-rich territory in the spring of 1981, looking for an estimated eight-day supply of oil for the U.S.A. The eight resultant dry holes were said by some ardent oil opponents to come directly from the hand of the Almighty.

Deciding such conflicts in court, case by case, has not led to a view of the whole, and two experienced coast defenders, quite independently of each other, say it never will. "Courts are not the forum," Sarah Bates, young lawyer at the Conservation Law Foundation, says. "Protection as opposed to exploitation must emerge from the political process." A colleague, Sarah Chasis, expert on coast matters at the National Resources Defense Council, questions dependence on the judicial system. "It doesn't work," she says.

"You cannot count solely on the courts, which are often slow-moving, or too deferential to the federal government, to resolve these issues properly."

It wasn't long before history proved them right. In 1983, Watt proposed the largest sale ever, 2.8 million acres over Georges and the deep canyons nearby where lobsters loiter in the dark. Even less oil was expected than before: the estimate of 123 million barrels was reduced to 50,000 barrels. Rumor had it that Watt's and the oil companies' insistence that Georges be made available anew was bravado to demonstrate that even minimum yield and maximum possibility for environmental damage could not shake them from their determination to keep the OCS leasing program intact. And the reason for *that*, New York's Governor Cuomo, suing to stop drilling off Long Island, suggests, is to get money to balance federal budget books before the 1984 presidential election.

One day before this second sale of Georges was to take place, it was enjoined by a Boston district court judge, to guarded rejoicing by the two Sarahs and coworkers. All are conscious that there is still not the necessary fact-supported long view to lend solid policy for the occasional enlightened judiciary to depend on. Without established policy, the oil chase will somehow, someday, again descend on Georges Bank.

Men are afraid to accept the end of oil's time on the planet, and get on with a future fuel. Fear leads to postponement of the end at any price, from the fish of Georges to the ancient culture of Norton Sound. We take no responsibility for the torrents of oil freed by digging in the OCS. By convolutions of logic it is all put down as an accident, and accidents are nobody's fault. The lasting effects of oil in sea-floor sediments are overlooked in the haste of the chase, although it is known that oil's poison eventually finds its way into fish flesh to threaten the life of whoever may eat it.

Thus it is that oil, the twentieth-century security blanket, is freed by man's hand to pollute its ocean creator. Here, on the loose, it contributes its tithe toward a killing sea.

6
THE SEA AS A SINK

The ocean has been pure and self-governing through the millions of years of its existence. Poets, children, and most of the rest of us have a firm, comforting image of the sea. Unchanging, accepting, it is big, beautiful, and full of surprises—huge toppling waves, currents grabbing at your feet, fish which find an exactly suitable niche in the holistic waters. The image has been so entrenched in our minds that in the last decades, man confidently proceeded with a serious intrusion into the ocean ecosystem, the dumping therein of modern wastes.

At first the ocean seemed unaffected. Then the amount of wastes intentionally put into it by the U.S. alone began to be measured in millions of tons. By the 1970s, it was more than 100 million tons. Some was biodegradable, able to be broken down into its components by the sea; some was not. Some accumulated in marine life, becoming more concentrated as it passed from plankton to predator along the food web. Some was toxic, causing adverse effects in fish. Some proved carcinogenic. The comforting image was somewhat shaken.

Then man-made toxic wastes were detected in the ocean's deepest deep. John Farrington of the Woods Hole Oceanographic Institution reports, "The quantities were very small: 10^{-10} grams per gram of marine organism tissue or oceanic sediment." But the chemicals, DDT and PCB, and radioactive fallout have been with us only for a few short decades. The ocean, known for its slow-moving personality, has speeded these poisons to the lowest spot in the world, a place from which there is no exit.

A startling find. These test-tube chemicals do not always break down fast in nature, if at all. Their presence in the deep sea, no matter how small the amount, means we have changed the ocean for as close to forever as man can measure. The change is in a contra-evolutionary direction. Marine biologist Dr. Howard Sanders, who has spent years studying the sea floor, explains: "The driving force of evolution is toward a finer adaptation of an organism to its environment. Toxic chemicals in the deep sea, where the environment has been constant over thousands of years, have the potential for a catastrophe." Jacques-Yves Cousteau puts it vividly: "If the sea continues to be used as our global sewer . . . we will undoubtedly bring upon ourselves catastrophe after catastrophe, ultimately depriving ourselves of the great resources of the sea. . . ." The consequences, he believes, "would read like a chapter out of Dante."

It is a shock to discover that what we dump in the sea penetrates so far, so fast. It is a shock that the habit of tossing wastes into the ocean has led us to dump the ultimate discard—radioactive waste—under the waves.

Its intimates call it hot garbage, or radwaste, diminutive for "radioactive waste." A radioactive substance is hot enough to give you cancer. You don't have to touch, breathe, or ingest its radiation; being exposed for a certain time and to a certain strength is enough. "Cancer is what cancer does. And cancer does kill," John Gofman, M.D., says in his authoritative *Radiation and Human Health*. There are many theories of how cancer starts, Gofman tells us, but the overwhelming scientific evidence is that radiation attacks one single normal cell, a microscopic entity. The cell holds genes, governors of body function, arranged in forty-six chromosomes. One of the most remarkable phenomena of life, Dr. Gofman says, is that when more cells are needed, a cell divides, recreating itself in exactly the right numbers and with exact replicas of the governing chromosomes.

Many cancer experts believe that cancer breaks the chromosome pattern and descendants of the changed cell repeat the alteration. If it is a reproductive cell, infants will carry the deformity. Unlike normal cell division, cancer allows unregulated, uncontrolled proliferation of the cell generations to follow. They do not necessarily divide faster, Dr. Gofman says, but they do keep dividing. Eventually, one way or another, they destroy their host.

Unbelievably, we put waste that can cause cancer in the ocean. What we are dumping now is low-level, that is, "anything other than high-level waste from a power plant," a Nuclear Regulatory Commission spokesman says. "An adequate definition of low-level nuclear waste does not exist," the Comptroller General's office says in 1983. Low-level waste includes discarded equipment, contaminated clothing, lab materials. One quarter comes from hospitals and universities, another quarter from industry, and almost half from commercial power plants. The radioactive waste rate of disintegration, generally called half-life, depends on its components, and varies from a few seconds to millions of years.

The assumption, back in the early dumping days, was that properly packaged radwaste deposited in the ocean was nothing to worry about. The evidence gives us pause. In 1976, an EPA oceanographer found ocean-floor sediments contaminated by radioactivity in both Atlantic and Pacific dumpsites. Survey voyages by EPA and NOAA (the National Oceanic and Atmospheric Administration) in 1982 retrieved bottom sediment samples with higher-than-expected levels of some long-lived isotopes—plutonium, cesium, and americum. Radioactivity, it seems, builds up in silt on the sea floor, suggesting that radwaste in the ocean can be disastrous.

Nevertheless, it has been dumped. Between 1946 and 1970, the United States deposited 90,000 concrete-lined drums of low-level radwaste at one dumpsite near the Farrallon Islands 50 miles off San Francisco, and at another dumpsite 130 miles off Sandy Hook, New Jersey. Recent searches located only a few hundred drums, some collapsed, some leaking. In the fifteen years before 1960, 4,000 canisters were put in the ocean 20 miles from Boston. This site, called Boston Foul Grounds, has the regrettable distinction, a witness told Congress, of being the shallowest water ever used for dumping atomic waste. By 1981, all the canisters had disappeared, location undiscovered.

A cloak-and-dagger footnote comes from a retired Navy pilot who tells officials that he flew three Atlantic dumping missions from Philadelphia in 1947. He had six tons of radwaste canisters aboard and orders to fly "low and slow" as he let them loose in the sea. Recently he went to check records of these missions. They were missing from the files.

Scuttling nuclear submarines is radwaste dumping in somewhat larger packages. The *Seawolf* was scuttled off Delaware in 1959 with its radioactive substance intact, and two other nuclear subs were lost in the 1960s. The Navy says radioactivity would decay before the steel which holds it corrodes, but some authorities say the Navy, being unable to find its ships, is guessing that this is the way it will be.

Before the Navy can receive its coveted new Trident subs, it has to get rid of its 120 obsolete nuclear submarines within thirty years. To sweeten the plan for disposing of them at sea, the Navy says the scuttling will be $2 million a ship cheaper than on land. It prepares a reassuring, soothing Environmental Impact Statement (EIS), promising that the subs' final resting places will be more than 2 miles down in the water where it is "cold, dark, and tranquil with a sparse population of organisms."

Read the fine print and you find that although the nuclear fuel would be removed before the final dive, the reactor compartment itself remains radioactive. It would be welded shut; "at least 200 years would pass before it would be penetrated by corrosion," the Navy says, still guessing. It does not mention troubling evidence of danger to the sea—the leaking drums, detectable levels of radioactivity in fish caught near the radwaste dumpsites, radioactive fallout in the deep. Nor does it speculate on the effect of eating fish or swimming in the sea at the start of the twenty-first century.

Several groups of activist environment protectors oppose the admirals. One group, Greenpeace, says the scuttled subs could emit high radioactivity. Greenpeace is determined to fight against subs' sea burial and believes ocean dumping of any kind of radwaste will open the door to more and more compromises by the U.S. and those nations which look to this country for policy.

There was a pause in radwaste dumping in the U.S. when amounts burgeoned, and packaging for ocean dumping became vastly expensive. Shallow land graves were substituted by 1970. Today, objections from neighbors of the grisly graveyards bring the nation full circle, back to dumping in the accepting sea where mermaids are the only constituents. We do not hear their voices.

The nation considers reinstating ocean dumping for low-level radwaste. Although a two-year moratorium swam into place, attached to a sure-to-pass congressional bill in the last hours of the 97th Congress, it is of dubious value, an impotent weapon as long as it remains unilateral. Great Britain, a long-time ocean dumper of radwaste, announced 4,200 tons scheduled for the North Atlantic in the summer of 1983. In May, 1983, the Swiss government says it would continue dumping low- and medium-level radwastes deep in the Atlantic. Japan prepares a large-scale ocean dumping program for radwaste; so, too, do Belgium and the Netherlands.

What happens next is of world concern. Because of the ocean's global nature, radwaste presses hard on the international conscience.

The nations of the world have promised each other not to put poisons in the ocean. That was back in 1975 when fifty-two states, the U.S. included, inaugurated the famous London Dumping

Convention (LDC), a signal that man, at that moment at least, had the collective vision to protect the sea in his own interest. Low-level radwaste dumping was allowed only with special permits. High-level waste was on the blacklist, prohibited along with other killers. In 1983, some of the nations agreed to an immediate global suspension of low-level radwaste dumping, pending scientific studies. The U.S., which had already passed its own moratorium, voted against this proposal for arcane reasons, and the U.K. and others followed its lead.

"The burden of proof that dumping is safe must be on the nations that dump or propose to dump," Clifton Curtis, of the Center of Law and Social Policy, says. "Otherwise, low-level radioactive waste must be totally prohibited." Curtis, who attended the meeting, was disappointed that the U.S. was not moving toward such a policy, and thought it should soon be in place to cope with whatever dangers would next appear. There was not long to wait.

None other than high-level nuclear wastes need a home. To date, no place on earth has been found which can be counted on to isolate radwaste from man and his food chain for the necessary million or more years. Tens of millions of gallons are stored on land in tanks which have already leaked badly. The pressure is on to find safe storage for what already exists, and all the gallons to come.

Eyes turn to the sea.

No container, however ingenious, could be made to resist corrosion of seawater for a million years. But it is thought that nature itself may have such a container in the deep seabed. Discovery, in the '60s, of the sea-floor structure, which revolutionized understanding of the workings of the globe, presents us with a new, intriguing dimension thousands of leagues under the sea. Here among the towering sea-floor mountains and deep trenches connecting to the globe's liquid core, there could be a place, some scientists believe, to isolate the killer waste.

More than 100 investigators from all over the nation are peering at a possible site under the aegis of the U.S. Department of Energy's Sandia National Laboratories. The object of their attention has been geologically stable for tens of millions of years, its low (2° C.) temperature varies less than a degree from day to day, millennium to millennium. The sea floor is unaffected by such shivering events as ice ages, miles above. Most important, Sandia scientists say, it is self-healing, a type of sediment made up of tiny grains packed tightly together in the water.

Abyssal red clay is the official name for this sediment, although it looks like chocolate-brown mud. Laid down some sixty-five million years ago, it covers almost a third of the sea floor, mostly in the open ocean, away from sea-floor action. "It seemed sensible to search for the least valuable piece of real estate on the planet," an important collaborator, Charles Hollister, Woods Hole scientist, says. If red clay turns out to be able to secure high-level radwaste for a million years or more, its value might switch from least to most.

Sandia is moving fast, has a national and international organization for the red clay connection, has scheduled a demonstration in the 1990s. Critics believe knowledge of the deep is too limited, that sediments are subject to slumping, erosion, and possible liquefaction, and that difficulties of transporting waste to its ocean bed are too dangerous. The ocean, some say, will return disposed radio-nuclides to man, invisible in seafood on the table.

The Ancients would have considered this a proper Neptunian rebuke. Gods were in business to protect nature. Homer relates a tale of Achilles throwing stacks of bloody corpses into the Scamender River, choking its flow and otherwise polluting it. The river's angered god raised a flood, threatening to drown Achilles and bury him in the river's sand and silt for his disregard. Early Persian religion protected nature even more devoutly. Earth, fire, and water were all sacred. No sewage could be put in the water, a scholar notes, no urine, excrement, even fingernail parings, and no dead bodies. Since earth and fire were off limits as well, corpses were simply exposed on bare rocks for disposition by wolves and vultures.

Cities grew. Sanctity of the elements was put aside in the struggle to solve the practicalities of urban life. Although waste was relatively simple, its disposal was a puzzlement then as now. Water seemed the optimum transport for wastes, and the sea the most convenient place for it to go. The ancients started building sewers, the most renowned being the Romans' stone-lined covered channel, Cloaca Maxima. Some public latrines and houses were connected to it, but many were not. With all its grandeur, Rome, it is said, smelled.

Getting rid of wastes has been a problem through the centuries. People ignored early ocean worship as they came to depend more and more on the sea as a sink. Where no sewers had been built, brooks and rivers, wandering through inland villages and towns, carried wastes seaward.

Dependence on the sea went unchallenged right up to the mid-twentieth century. In Nieuw Amsterdam, for example, sewage was collected in pails and dumped into nearby rivers. Modern-day Broad Street, first a brook, then a canal, became the city's first Common Sewer in 1680. Soon the waters around the city were contaminated, and by the start of this century, the sewage of 3.5 million people, flowing raw into the Bronx, Harlem, and other New York City rivers, transformed them into open sewers and the harbor into a virulent health hazard. Because the harbor silted up fast, it needed frequent dredging to keep it open to shipping, and the resulting dredge spoils were a problem of bulk and contamination.

Effects of sewage and dredging came out of the closet almost a hundred years ago when two major fisheries felt their ill effects. The shad catch declined from 4 million pounds in 1895 to a tenth of that amount in 1905, an early city sewage commission noted. The thriving oyster and clam business collapsed under the impact of dumping and dredging. A severe blow was the linkage of contaminated shellfish to the city's typhoid cases. Shellfish beds were closed by 1921 and still are. Fewer varieties of fish and shellfish were able to survive the increasingly polluted water. Exact records are skimpy because most early biologists, a contemporary says, spent their time discovering and classifying the new world's species rather than noting their decline.

Using the sea as a sink was a well-entrenched idea. When trouble came, any thought of giving up this convenience, however dangerous to health, was inconceivable. Instead, when the harbor had deteriorated to critical levels, attention focused on alleviating matters by building sewers and sewage treatment plants. This answer could not catch up with the problem. The city's population boomed; the volume of sewage multiplied. Even if all of it could have been safely disposed of, sewage was not the only villain. The Industrial Age had arrived. Waste changed.

Neptune would be in a towering rage at what we now put into the ocean. More waste goes into the New York Bight than any other single place in the U.S.A., making it one of the most severely degraded ocean areas in the world, Don Walsh of the National Advisory Committee on Oceans and Atmosphere (NACOA) says. A hard look at this big city's acute water-connected distress provides a preview into what is ahead for coastal cities elsewhere—and for the sea.

A piece of the ocean 12 miles equidistant from the shores of New York and New Jersey is the dumpsite shared by these neighbors. Into its 30-meter depth, huge amounts of dredge spoil and sludge slide off the barges lying low in the water under their loads. An estimated 8 billion gallons of municipal sewage is discharged each day into U.S. coastal waters. A considerable fraction reaches the New York Bight, and the amount increases 2 to 3 percent each year. The sludge increased from 4 million tons to 7 million tons per year from 1977 to 1980. EPA estimates that, at this rate, by 1987 there will be 9 million tons of it dumped into the Bight. Part of this sludge comes from New Jersey, where some 15,000 companies produce more than a million gallons of liquid chemical wastes per year along with 3 million tons of industrial waste. It is more toxic than New York's waste, due to the industrial input.

Sewage sludge is a virulent concentration of the new look in waste. John Farrington and fellow scientists describe it as containing solid human waste, viruses and pathogenic bacteria, known or potentially toxic, mutagenic, and carcinogenic chemicals such as PCB, DDT, heavy metals. Some persist in the ocean. "The net result is that sludge contains elevated concentrations of toxic chemicals," Farrington says. This is no mere sewage.

Sludge comes from rainfall, from the city streets, some from sewage treatment plants, some straight from the toilet (about half of New York's sewage is untreated). In sludge there are man-made chemicals called organohalogens, persistent and highly toxic to people and to marine life. Among the first in wide use was the insecticide DDT. Found guilty of causing silent springs by Rachel Carson and others, it was banned, only to be succeeded by less familiar but sometimes more damaging compounds. The best known threat came from deadly PCB, an industrial compound invented in 1929, used in the electric industry and now also banned from manufacture.

We learn nothing. There are dozens of competitors already invented to again pass along the killer mantle.

Oil and grease in sludge contain the toxic petroleum compounds known as polycyclic aromatic hydrocarbons, or PAH. Eating PAH-contaminated fish or shellfish is another cancer risk, can cause abnormal cell growth, birth defects in offspring. Fish do not have the instinct to stay away from PAHs.

The heavy metals in sludge, such as mercury, lead, copper and cadmium, also accumulate in marine organisms and poison humans who eat the contaminated seafood, as in the unforgettable Minimata event. Some metals have recently been found to interact with coliform bacteria from human excrement in sludge. The bacteria is then resistant to its natural killer, able to survive where

it once was prey to antibacterial agents. Exposure to these strength-
ened bacteria by eating fish or shellfish leads to seriously drug-
resistant disease. Over the long term, drug-resistant bacteria are on
the increase.

Dilution, dispersion, sedimentation, and degradation—these
are the four horsemen which carry the banner of ocean dumpers.
Some of the four diminish some of the waste. But some elements
of waste, as has been seen, stay in the water long enough to cause
trouble, building what has been described as "insidious reservoirs"
in sediment and shellfish. Oil, heavy metals, man-made chemicals, and the rest have longer water lives than we might wish. A
virulent example is the collection of more than 100 viruses in human waste, the enteric viruses. What happens to them in the sea
is now the subject of detailed research, chiefly at the University of
Minnesota.

Water that tests "clean" on a bacteria count may be home to
clams, crabs, mussels, widely infected by these viruses. At a Philadelphia dumpsite, seventeen months after sludge dumping there
had stopped, the viruses were isolated. Their survivability in the
sea creates a newly recognized sludge hazard. They not only live
much longer than expected but also survive cooking. A study of
the polio virus, for example, shows that even after baking, stewing,
frying, and steaming its shellfish host, 7 to 10 percent of the virus
was still viable, ready to attack the next gastrointestinal tract preparing to digest it.

The enteric virus spectrum is worth attention. It stretches from
the polio virus which can give you meningitis, paralysis, fever, to
hepatitis type A to Coxsackie virus which causes nyocarditis, respiratory disease, and a considerable list of other horrors. "Waterborne disease outbreaks are no longer on the decline in this country," the investigators say. Although there is less typhoid, there is
more infectious hepatitis and there is a firm correlation between
swimming in sludge-polluted waters and severe attacks of gastroen-
teritis.

There were twenty-two outbreaks connected with eating shell-fish in New York State during the summer of 1982. Five hundred people had severe nausea and diarrhea; there were ten cases of hepatitis A. The state's health commissioner issued an advisory warning against eating raw clams and oysters. Shellfish that could be traced came from Rhode Island, Massachusetts, Long Island, New York. A large amount were illegally harvested, a very profit-able undertaking, the New York Department of Health comments.

If sludge were all, we might invent a way for safe disposal. There are efforts to use decontaminated sludge as fertilizer or to disperse it into the atmosphere by burning. We can decide where to put this potent waste and put it there. This is not true of the waste which without our help pours into the harbor from rivers, their courses lined with industry and power plants which dump all manner of chemicals into the obliging stream. Sand and mud at the harbor's mouth are a receptive sponge for contamination from rivers, from city streets, and from the harbor that once beckoned to Henry Hudson with its serene beauty and "the scent of many wilde flowers on the aire."

For New York harbor to continue as a convenient port, it needs to be dredged, being otherwise too shallow. The vastest bulk of all waste is the dredge spoil removed from harbors such as this. It is a colossal 80 percent of all ocean dumping.

In the late 1970s New York was the largest American port. In one year some 7,600 oceangoing vessels edged past the Statute of Liberty into the harbor, their safe landing made possible by the Corps of Engineers' huge dredging program. The dredge spoil is moved to a site off New Jersey, called, appropriately enough, the Mud Dump. "The Corps estimates that 10 percent . . . is clean sand and that less than 10 percent is so highly contaminated that it is not suitable for open-water disposal," a panel discussion on Dredged Material Management says. It recommends alternatives, their fate still undecided.

Ocean dumping has long been a commonly held privilege,

untrammeled except for the 1890 Rivers and Harbors Act, which barred "deposition of refuse," i.e., garbage dumping. The law regulated only solids. Amazingly, it was not until the 1960s that we started to examine the effects of dumping on the fauna and waters of the New York Bight. The threats to marine life, and to man, inspired President Nixon to order up a study of ocean dumping from his Council on Environmental Quality.

The result was a Neptune-minded law to regulate ocean dumping of materials adverse to health and to the marine ecology. The Marine Protection, Research and Sanctuaries Act of 1972, known as the Ocean Dumping Act, was the first important law of the land to worry about the continuing integrity of the sea around us.

With this law in its pocket, the U.S. helped fifty-two governments to agree to the 1973 London Dumping Convention. It is still beyond the nations of the world to wholeheartedly endorse it. But committing to paper global responsibility for preserving the natural state of the ocean is a step. It will make history if we use it well, history of a different kind if we fail to.

Back at home in the mid-1970s, the ocean dumping law was having its own troubles. Scientists' views were far apart. Some argued that the ocean could safely accept enormous volumes of wastes, calling again on the reliable four horsemen—dilution, dispersion, sedimentation, and degradation—to prove their point. Others piled up facts never before assembled of poisons accumulating in the sea. Then, unexpectedly, the public was heard from, loud and clear.

In the Bicentennial summer of 1976, celebrating East Coast citizens were treated to a fouling of Long Island beaches by sewage and a massive fish kill down the coast. It was the first of what is now expected to be a never-ending series of coast disasters as the ocean rises up in protest against intrusion. The resultant public uproar was an outpouring of fear that the torrents of sewage would never stop. A New Jersey congressman proposed to amend the U.S. Ocean Dumping Law with an absolute ban on all sewage sludge dumping—deadline December 31, 1981. Political pressures forced a two-word compromise—a ban against ocean dumping which would *unreasonably degrade* the waters.

How much degradation is reasonable, if any? To decide requires a philosophy—how long do we want a viable ocean?—and information on effects of waste. Neither exists. Three outstanding scientists edited an important collection of current knowledge, *Ocean Dumping of Industrial Wastes*: Messrs. Bostwick Ketchum of Woods Hole (before his untimely death), Dana Kester from the University of Rhode Island, and P. Kihlo Park of NOAA, who wrote the windup chapter. The ban, they say, "was based more on ignorance about the possible consequences of ocean dumping than on knowledge that such waste disposal was detrimental to society's overall use of the oceans." The ban was a rare look-before-you-leap action. Before we proceed with waste disposal, it suggests, let's find out its effects. It is, the authors say, "a major challenge to the understanding of the marine processes. We do not know the capacity of these pelagic oceanic regions to assimilate wastes without detrimental effects."

Before the ink was dry on this sober encouragement of an all-out research effort, the U.S. reversed the policy of its 1970s law to protect the ocean. In the early 1980s, it decided that the ocean *could* absorb some of the wastes the nation produced, not only could, but should, share the troublesome burden with earth and air, now given the brisk modern title "media."

There was a new presidential advisory, this time from the chief executive's NACOA. It proposed that the dumping ban be lifted and waste disposed of by "a multimedia approach . . . in the manner and medium that minimizes the risk to human health and the environment, and at a price that this nation is prepared to pay." Regulators would have to know what waste would do to whichever "medium" was contemplated for disposal, compared for risk and cost to other disposal options. Given the slower-than-earth pace of ocean reactions, it was a virtually impossible assignment. But wastes have to go somewhere, NACOA tells the president and Congress. If there are risks in using the ocean, we do not know exactly what they are and it may be decades, centuries, before we do know. The sense of the report is that wherever we put our wastes, we are taking a risk, so we might as well use the ocean. A little more danger, a little less. . . .

The law to stop dumping by the end of 1981 was still in force. Some cities, notably Philadelphia, had obeyed it. Called the City of Brotherly Sludge by its downstream neighbors, it was sued by the EPA in 1978 for dumping violations. Philadelphia met the ocean dumping deadline by switching to land disposal. New York, biggest dumper of all, did not. "As Mayor of a City with over seven million residents living in a very small space and abutting the ocean," Mayor Koch tells Congress, "I want to make certain that adequate protections, based on the best scientific evidence available, exist to protect [our natural resources]." The mayor said the land-based alternative that consultants had designed would be temporary, and would cost $335 million to construct.

Instead, New York sued the Environmental Protection Agency (EPA), charged with carrying out the law. In the spring of 1981, Judge Abraham Sofaer of the U.S. District Court decided that EPA had misinterpreted the law. The compromise, "unreasonably degrade," was the swing phrase. "Had Congress intended to require an absolute end to all ocean dumping," Judge Sofaer's opinion says, "the phrase would have been unnecessary." The Judge finds EPA failed in its duty to evaluate all manner of disposal and choose the least harmful and least expensive.

The EPA read its charge from the amended Ocean Dumping Act as a mandate to stop ocean dumping. It had found New York's dumping did unreasonably degrade the waters of New York Bight, if presenting the next generations with a surviving ocean is the intent of the law.

Judge Sofaer apparently read the same legislation as a command to evaluate waste disposal on land, in the air, and in the sea, and find the least harmful, most economic method of getting rid of it. He followed, indeed quoted, the precepts suggested by the presidential-advisory NACOA. This brief effort to protect the ocean was over. New York City "won."

"Banning Ocean Dumping: So Near but Yet Sofaer" is the cry. The EPA did not appeal the Sofaer decision. Administrator Gorsuch, before her departure, had so reduced the Agency's staff and budget that it could not keep up with its increasing burdens. Any thought that the EPA might undertake the huge task of an overall waste disposal plan vanished. Even hopes for research and monitoring renewed ocean dumping disappeared. NOAA has "deferred projects which would assess sewage disposal effects and human health risks to budget outyears," an official says, indicating that "outyears" are somewhere beyond the horizon. Further, its 1983 budget for these matters has been cut exactly in half. The happy talk of comparing media risks and costs is fast forgotten.

Ocean dumping is on the rise again. New York, triumphant in what its lawyers may call a victory, six New Jersey authorities, and Washington, D.C., have formally filed for permits. South Essex, Massachusetts, follows the same course. NOAA estimates a 300 percent increase in localities which will apply for ocean dumping permits, given an emasculated EPA and Sofaer's green light. The London Convention is conveniently ignored, was not mentioned by either party in the New York versus EPA argument, although it binds the U.S.A. not to put poisons in the world sea.

The popular idea now is that there is an amount of waste which we can dump without harming the ocean or ourselves. This is called the ocean's assimilative capacity. No one knows what it may be or how to find out. True, there are the four horsemen which dilute, disperse, sink, and degrade, able to hide pollutants. But we know that this ocean quartet cannot detroy the indestructibles we add to the vast seas. To believe that the ocean has a capacity—a threshold—which can be calculated, and that we can pollute up to that threshold, but not beyond, is an absurdity.

"Small changes have small effects, but effects nevertheless," George Woodwell, distinguished marine biologist at Woods Hole tells a visitor. "You can pick up one part per quadrillion of PCB. Add another small amount, and another, and soon we'll have large amounts and large effects. What's the assimilative capacity? None." Woodwell is dedicated to the physical, chemical, and biotic integrity of the ocean waters. "The assimilative capacity," he says succinctly, "is fiction."

The ocean, having no human inhabitants, is not protected like the land, where governors, mayors, and administrators reign. But it has innate power. Toxics put into the ocean may be whisked away to the deep, to reappear when caught up by a fish or a current. They may be banked in sediments; they may combine with some seawater element or other, creating a new ocean danger. The ocean insult, be it low-level radwaste or PCB, with few exceptions shows itself at the slow, deliberate pace of the ocean. We may not see the results in days, years, even in our own lifetimes. We can only guess where and how the ocean accumulates the insolubles we deliberately add to its waters, and what the ultimate effects will be.

The ocean might be suggesting, more and more forcibly, that man devise a different sink. Or find a way to eliminate the need for one.

7

THE SEA
ALSO RISES

The peaceful blue ocean seems a world apart from the world which powers this fuel-hungry era. We do not easily connect irregular behavior of the ocean—erosion of our shore, floods in unexpected profusion—to the burning of more and more oil and coal. But the vast sea and the increase in energy consumption now collide and lock in geologic interaction. The result is terrifying. The world is getting hotter and the seas are on the rise.

Scientific research, brilliant, dogged, escorts us into the fast-approaching hot climate. Whether we will be able to work, stay healthy, enjoy life, has yet to be determined. So has the new pattern of growing food. In the U.S., rainfall might move northward, leaving an arid Midwest behind. All over the world, change in place and type of food production has been followed by famine, and mass migrations. This time there will be less land to move to. The ocean will rise, perhaps high enough to melt the great glaciers, drowning the lowlands of the world and covering a lot of valuable real estate with a warming rising sea. It will batter the concrete footings of vast coast cities, topple towers, and chase coast dwellers into the hills.

Until now, the ocean has had the awesome capacity to stabilize climate. In combination with the sun, atmosphere, and the mantle of life which wraps the globe, the ocean creates a climate to keep our planet habitable, and has done so for all the years that life has existed. It collects solar heat in clear tropical waters, stores it in mid-latitudes, radiates it in polar regions, moving it by current and wind. It responds slowly to the sun; the top layers, weeks behind change on land, are warm in autumn, cold in spring. The ocean is likely to lag years behind larger changes in global temperature. The temperature of the deep is believed to take 1,000 years to change.

Over the long sweep of time, climate changes. The earth has been warm and moist; it has been half-covered with ice; it has been temperate as it is now. Climate, awesome in its power, is arranged in a surprisingly delicate balance, evolving slowly enough to give life forms time to adjust over many generations. Fool around with this balance and you are likely to stir the giant to unpredictable action.

We are doing exactly that. We are warming up the globe. Most scientists agree that the average global temperature is increasing because of man. From the National Center for Atmospheric Research, investigators predict that before 2020, the world will be 1.8° warmer than now, warmer, in fact, than it has been at any time in the past 1,000 years. (All temperatures are Fahrenheit, as you see them on your home thermometer except where noted. Fahrenheit is 1.8° for each degree Celsius.) The temperature in Boston will be like Washington, D.C. today; Copenhagen like Paris. In the second stage of warming that will follow, according to these calculations, Boston will approach the mean temperature of Miami; the southern parts of the U.S. and Europe will be truly tropical. The Council on Environmental Quality (CEQ) believes the temperature will increase between 2.7° and 8.1° by the mid-twenty-first century, and most other estimates are in this range.

In the 1980s, there is no urgency to be the first on your block to buy an igloo in the Arctic. But there is every reason to understand the predicted warming and make decisions with that future in mind. A great deal is tentative, a great deal still unknown. There has never been a man-made change in the global climate before.

It is alarming that so little is known, leaving so much to projections based on natural climate changes in the past. Complete proof is still lacking; global research is far from robust. The change will not be measurable for about fifteen years. The formidable Catch-22 is that if we wait for incontrovertible proof of climate change, in all probability it will already be inevitable and irreversible. Where it will take us, nobody knows.

There are those who hang back from the startling fact of global warming, waiting for proof to pile higher. Meanwhile they continue to accept the status quo, hoping not to have to face another environmental horror. "Show me," they say about the warming as about the effects of caustic acid rain or toxic waste, thus postponing the day of reckoning.

Men of a different mind are able to look ahead to a changed ocean circumstance, try to measure it, understand it, plan for it. Investigation is under way all over the world. In many places scientists labor, looking back and ahead, uncovering clues, amassing data.

They are looking at a crucial element of the climate system, a transparent gas well known to this society—carbon dioxide. A modest amount of this CO_2 is evenly spread out in the atmosphere and the sun's rays pass through it freely to the earth. But infrared heat rays which bounce back from earth, headed toward outer space, are mostly blocked by the CO_2, keeping the heat in the atmosphere to warm the world. Less than 10 percent escapes to space. Without CO_2 the ocean would freeze; with too much CO_2 it would boil itself away. This so-called greenhouse effect was initiated when the world began.

For billions of years, CO_2 has spurted into the atmosphere from the core of the globe through volcanoes which erupt often enough to keep the sky well supplied. Roger Revelle, former director of the Scripps Institution of Oceanography in La Jolla, California, who has spent years investigating CO_2, says that 50 million gigatons (a gigaton is a billion tons) have entered the atmosphere this way, about 40 million tons a year. If it had all stayed in the sky, the earth's surface temperature would be many hundred degrees hotter, much like that of Venus where 98 percent of the atmosphere is CO_2. There the temperature, Revelle says, is "a hellish 400°C" (752°F).

Earth triumphs over such as Venus because of its ocean, the only known ocean in the universe. The ocean is able to absorb most of the CO_2 from the atmosphere, leaving behind the 700 gigatons required for the heat-saving function. The rate at which the ocean can absorb extra CO_2 is the rate at which we can safely burn the fossil fuels which release it.

CO_2 is an active, slightly acidic gas. When it meets the surface of the ocean, it reacts with what it finds there. It is immediately used for vital photosynthesis, then must descend through the water column to the cavernous storehouse of the deep. Here it is eventually deposited on the ocean floor, some as calcium carbonate to be used for shells and skeletons. Over time, some of the 50 million gigatons became fossil fuels—coal, oil, gas—buried in rock for a quarter of a billion years or more. When they were discovered, man chose to burn them, providing himself with heat and power and releasing the carbon once again. The burning put carbon dioxide right back into the atmosphere from whence it came.

Almost a century ago, two scientists independently discovered carbon dioxide's remarkable ability to absorb radiation from the earth. Each published this startling news in scientific journals to a curiously indifferent world. Perhaps nobody then imagined the day that this exquisitely tidy heating system might be thrown off balance by the human occupants of the globe. But in 1938, when S. S. Callendar, a British engineer, noted that CO_2 was increasing in the atmosphere, he attracted worldwide attention. He didn't expect it; "Few of those familiar with the natural heat exchange of the atmosphere would be prepared to admit that the activities of man could have any influence upon a phenomenon on so vast a scale."

In the late 1950s data began to be assembled. Carbon dioxide in the atmosphere started to be monitored at the Mauna Loa Observatory on an Hawaiian volcano rim, in Alaska, the South Pole, Sweden. All agree on the mounting curve that "looks like a cobra

ready to strike," one scientist said. CO_2 in the atmosphere increased 8 percent between the start of monitoring and 1983; it has
increased approximately 26 percent since the start of the Industrial
Revolution. This latter figure might change. George Woodwell,
working on the CO_2 problem at the Marine Biological Laboratory
at Woods Hole, says the world's biota, particularly its forests, release enough carbon to have "important implications for estimat-
ing the seriousness of the CO_2 increase." Carbon dioxide, Woodwell says, "may rapidly become a major threat to the present world
order." He will soon propose a new calculation of its growth in the
atmosphere since the mid-nineteenth century. It was then 280 parts
per million (ppm), many say. In 1983 it was 340 ppm. Woodwell's
new figure will present a lower start, faster rise.

Most research points to a doubling of preindustrial CO_2 in the
atmosphere in the twenty-first century. Then, the temperature will
rise 5.4°; at higher latitudes, the rise will be between 12.6° and
18°. It will be a hotter world than has prevailed for the last several
thousand years. "The CO_2 issue may present the ultimate environmental dilemma," says Gus Speth, who, as chairman of the CEQ,
edited its report on the subject in 1980. "Every effort should be
made to ensure that nations are not compelled to choose between
the risks of energy shortages and the rise of CO_2." If we keep on
increasing our use of fossil fuels at the present 2.2 percent a year,
the doubling will occur at around 2060. If we hold use at its present level, the doubling will be postponed to 2175 or thereabouts.

It could get even hotter than predicted. Warmer air over the
ocean makes more water vapor, and it also retains heat from the
globe, pushing the temperature up. Release of other gases such as
methane and chlorofluorocarbons will have an additional warming
effect, 50 percent to 100 percent that of CO_2, a recent report says.
As Woodwell tells us, cutting down forests where CO_2 is stored
also releases the gas, although the amount is hard to compute. We
do know for sure that fossil fuel burning is the main source and
the ocean the main sink for the extra CO_2 in the sky.

For a time the reaction to this growing assemblage of data was at best apathetic. The general assumption was that such a problem had not happened before, and so it could not happen now, that in any event the ocean would take care of excess CO_2.

The assumption is wrong. Although there is thought to be plenty of room for CO_2 in the capacious regions of the deep, the process of getting it there forestalls instant storage. If the ocean has gotten warmer—and it is exceedingly hard to take its temperature—it absorbs CO_2 more slowly. If the top ocean layers are saturated with CO_2, there is a further delay until it can descend through the water column.

We may pass the point of no return long before bougainvillas bloom in Boston. We have not felt the heat yet because of nature's trick of slowing the warming in the sea. "Finding the signal in the noise," the CEQ says, "is an extraordinarily difficult dilemma. . . ."

Skeptics are pleased to point to abnormally cold winter months or freezing days, ignoring the critical difference between weather—short-term and local—and climate, which changes over centuries and is a collection of weathers. Climate-minded scientists comparing trends of fifty, one hundred years or centuries, millennia, thus remain unshaken by the short cooling period between 1940 and 1965, caused by certain natural phenomena which were strong enough to override the still-young warming trend.

Short-term climate extremes of one kind or another lead us to "overlook the in-built trap in the nature of the climate problem," H. H. Lamb, renowned British climatologist, points out in his encyclopedic *Climate, History and the Modern World*. "The wide range of year-to-year variations will always make it hard to recognize any new trend until it is firmly established." Lamb's particularly cautious forecast is for a warming, increasing over the next century to a peak around 2100.

Among the very first bits of evidence that the warming has begun was a measured decrease in Antarctic pack ice in the 1970s

104

as compared with the 1930s. Temperature in the melt area was almost 1.8° higher in the '70s than in the '30s, George Kukla and Joyce Gavin of Columbia University reported in 1981 to the National Science Foundation, which financed their work. "It's exciting," Kukla said. "This is just where we expected the warming element to be."

If you read this when the temperature is below zero and the snow flies, remember the "in-built trap" and rely on assembled scientific data, more each day, which leads most scientists to agree that the warming is under way. Keep your perspective and read scare headlines with a knowing eye. "Earth Said to Be in 'Icehouse' "; Walter Sullivan's article under this misleading title reports some recent evidence of times when the world has been hotter than it is today. What he fails to say is news. The difference between the present warming and the long series of such happenings is that for the first time the globe heats up at man's hand and man's pace, faster than nature's pace at any time in history.

A few natural climate changes are on the record. A sudden advance of ice around 10,000 years ago killed living forests wholesale in less than a century, one investigator says. More doleful is "the time of great dying" at the end of the Mesozoic era some 65 million years ago when some believe that many dinosaur species became extinct. Dewey McLean, geologist at Virginia Polytechnic Institute, has a theory, interesting if less than widely accepted, that there was a massive natural killing of a certain plankton, which released CO_2 into the air, causing an abrupt ocean warming and a hotter environment. Most dinosaurs, accustomed to the climate of the era, could not adapt to the heat fast enough and soon died out, leaving their record in marine microfossils, a kindly warning to humans of what a repeat of such a sudden warming might mean. Will future earth creatures marvel at *our* skeletons in a museum just as we take our children to gaze at bones of the once dominant great beasts?

Dr. Jerome Weisner, president emeritus of the Massachusetts

Institute of Technology, is impressed with the seriousness of the CO_2 warming. He sees it as a global dilemma. "It means getting the world to agree to a change to non-fossil fuel," Dr. Weisner said in an interview. In four or five months during 1983, he had become more convinced than ever that there is "only a short time left to make a long-term plan. It needs lots of inventiveness." As an example, Dr. Weisner described an idea for power plants to be built on the coast, with huge pipes to carry carbon dioxide waste directly into the depths of the sea where there is plenty of room for carbon storage. Thus the atmosphere, where there is no room, would be undisturbed.

Such positive thinking combats the present denial of the fact that by our own action we are building up to the beginning of a Venusian future. If we postpone efforts to ameliorate this trend, we risk sudden acquisition of a way of life we know nothing about, at a temperature which our bodies might require more time to adapt to than there will be.

Most natural climate change happened gradually, over centuries. Our ancestors left the caves which protected them from the rigors of the Ice Age over many generations, following their food supply of wild animals, which slowly moved down into the sunshine of valleys freed of the freeze. Tribes migrated out of plains which were turning to deserts. Agriculture, lifestyle, place of habitation were inexorable but gentle climate dictates over generations. Slowly, new settlements clustered where the climate was suitable to growing crops, houses were built to protect against the environment, perhaps thatched straw huts to shade from the sun, perhaps tightly fitted stone to keep out the cold.

Migration is the classic response to droughts, desertifications, or other alteration of the ability to grow food. The Irish potato famine and migration to the U.S. is a recent example. Economists and population experts see little chance of mass migrations continuing in the modern crowded world. But, right now, a large-scale move away from floods and encroaching water, away from unaccustomed heat might be needed. It will be more feasible if experts go to work, finding where there are vacant cool mountains and what might be designed there for the twenty-first-century refugees.

Unless we find a substitute for fossil fuels in time, there will be no chance to isolate ourselves from the day-to-day weather by air-conditioning and/or heating. Turn up the air-conditioner and you put even more CO_2 into the atmosphere, bring more heat to the earth.

Glacier Lake in Alaska, surrounded by ice-covered mountains, reflects the blue of deep ice with occasional clear aquamarine depths. It harbors icebergs which have the unnerving habit of crackling with sudden deep rumbles as pieces break away to float in independent vastness. Glaciers here seem timeless, part of an enormous design in which mankind is dwarfed to insignificance. Now, unimaginably, man may dominate the glacial future.

We live in an Ice Age, albeit during one of its interglacial periods, the same that accounted for Herodotus' shell. The fact that glaciers now exist is a majestic if chilly reminder that the Ice Age continues. This is the most recent of the four ice epochs; it started fifteen million years ago. It has advanced and retreated every 100,000 years for the past three million years, and attained its maximum 20,000 years ago, when the amount of ice covering this continent, scientist Cesare Emiliani says, was "truly phenomenal." It took 100,000 years to form, a tenth of that time to melt. It reached down to parallel 37°N in North America (San Francisco, Washington, D.C.), 50°N in Europe (Frankfurt, Prague), its glacial ice sheets blanketing mountains and plains. Spruce forests grew in Florida and Texas, musk oxen lived in the central U.S., and giant icebergs visited the English Channel.

Water to make this ice could come only from the sea. Thus depleted, the ocean was 300 feet lower than it is now. Continental shelves were exposed, mastodons and maybe humans lived 125 miles off the present coastline.

When the ice sheet started to give way, some 17,000 years

ago, it thinned first, then melted around the edges. Water poured off the continents, the seas rose. Coasts receded (we call it erosion) often in sudden bursts set off by great storms. H. H. Lamb believes that Ice Age people were generally coast dwellers and that many, unable to migrate quickly enough, were drowned by the sudden sea rise. "The end of the Ice Age and the continued rise of sea level that followed may have greatly reduced the numbers of mankind—an event rare in history—and given rise to many legends of a great flood in ancient times."

Geologic research turns up evidence of enormous destructive floods everywhere on the globe. As is often the case, such common events were told in stories by the evening fire and passed down from one generation to the next. Floods show up in Greek, Babylonian, and Hindu folklore. One account was discovered in 1850 on a tablet in cuneiform script unearthed at the site of Nineveh. It tells the story of Gilgamesh, the ancient king, who achieved immortality by surviving a flood. The Mesopotamian flood in the fourth or fifth century B.C., the Old Testament tells us, is the time when rain fell for forty days and forty nights to destroy mankind for its wickedness.

A truly universal flood, affecting all mankind and all the coasts of the world, can happen only if the floor of the ocean rises or ice on the land melts, Emiliani says. It is intriguing that geologists, who know most about these world disasters, call such a flood a "transgression." There are two notable transgressions in history, one eighty million years ago; another, the largest and most widespread, 450 million years back. In the U.S. "only present-day Minnesota and Wisconsin, western Montana and northern Idaho, and small areas of Colorado and the Southwest, remained above water," one account says. Prehistoric shorelines have been found in the mountains of Minnesota, mute evidence that the sea rose to mountain heights during the biggest transgression of them all.

Noah's flood in 2350 B.C., according to Biblical chronology, was probably not a true transgression. It could have been a prototype, an oft-repeated memory enlarged in the telling, or a local happening which seemed of great importance to those who experienced it and survived to tell the tale. Or there could have been a proper deluge, an ark-like craft, and enough pairs of animals to make the vivid story everlasting. There are many theories, no proof. We only know that floods were part of the general experience in those ice-melting days.

They will be again.

These glimpses of sea level rising and falling through time defy our comfortable assumption of a stable shoreline. A changing coast is unfamiliar because it usually happens very slowly, more slowly than could be encompassed in a lifetime. A fraction of an inch, even one whole inch, was thought incidental, if bothersome. The rise of the Atlantic sea level, now at the rate of about 12 to 15 inches average per century, according to Orrin Pilkey, geologist, worries landholders who build defenses against the rising sea or spend small fortunes to renourish their treasured share of the shore with imported sand. They like to believe that their troubles are caused by erosion, a temporary plague that will soon cease.

The ladder to the beach has been ripped off its underpinnings and scattered like so much kindling. What remains extends into air, a reminder of the bank that has been lost to the sea. Carefully tended pines and beach roses hang by a root; the picnic cove has vanished. It is as though some furious giant trampled through the neighborhood, ripping up man's hopes for a lifetime oceanside retreat. Elsewhere, houses topple, giving way to the waves. No one had much noticed that the sea was higher than before. No one much believed that the million-dollar coast would be snatched from them, suddenly, over a winter. They question what can be done to preserve it. They will find it hard to believe that the giant who did the deed is us.

The sea's vertical peregrinations are no longer mysterious. It has been discovered that climate and sea level are one system, indivisible. Climate, warming at its new, fast, man-made rate, will

109

warm the sea. In our lifetime, air and sea will get hotter as CO_2 accumulates in the atmosphere, and this will cause the sea level to rise. In the kettle on the stove, water expands as it heats and it does the same in the ocean. Volume enlarges as temperature goes up.

The other source of a rising sea is water released from melting glaciers and from the colossal West Antarctic ice sheet. One hundred twenty-five thousand years ago was the last time it melted, flooding low coasts all over the world. The world temperature has risen to exactly what it was at that melting. No one knows how much longer West Antarctic ice will resist the warming globe.

Some day it could disintegrate in a few hundred years of higher temperatures, raising the sea level twenty feet. If all the glaciers in Antarctica and Greenland melt, the sea level would rise a breathtaking 150 to 300 feet, scientists say. As far as is known, this remarkable event would take hundreds of years.

The ocean plunges us into a world where we have lost control of our surroundings. Unlike the wilderness on land that pioneers "tamed" to suit themselves, the ocean tames us with its fast, apparently inexorable rise. The global sea level rises somewhat more slowly than Pilkey's figure for the U.S. Atlantic coast. Globally the rise has been 4 to 6 inches in the past century. It could rise 8 inches per year by the year 2000, 4 feet by 2050, 12 feet by 2100. This is the "high" scenario assembled by experts brought together for a sea rise conference in the spring of '83, by the U.S. Environmental Protection Agency (EPA).

As the expanding sea moves against the shore, it will drown low-lying areas where there is least resistance to its pressure. A rise of 4 feet, the EPA report says, will flood major portions of Louisiana and Florida, as well as resorts irreverently perched on dunes and beaches on the Gulf and Atlantic coasts. Marshes lying on bays, sounds, along riverbanks close to the sea, will also be submerged, a major tragedy for the marine ecosystem. Marshes manufacture food for marine life with an incredibly well-designed system, using the abilities of sun, water, and spartina grass, a saltwater resident,

110

with tides for transport of ingredients in, the finished product out. Marshes are a nursery for some species, a permanent home for others. They also act as a huge sponge, absorbing excess waters, protecting uplands from floods. It takes hundreds of years for marshes to grow and there is, to date, no replacement for these natural engineering wonders. Their loss will endanger the continuing existence of fish and people.

Coastlines high enough to avoid flooding are pushed inland. Before the present sea rise, winter storms washed sand from beaches offshore, then redeposited it in gentler spring and summer weather. We haven't caught up with the facts of a rising sea; "Life in Los Angeles: Waiting for the Sea to Give Back the Sand" is a 1983 headline. Most believe that although severe storms have recently wrecked much of California's 1,000-mile coastline, damaged beach homes, and left piles of gray pebbles where there once were wide, smooth beaches, the sand will return as it always has.

With deeper water offshore, the washed-away sand will not return. It is required in the water, experts say, to preserve the shore-sea relationship. The beach is sacrificed to rising waters.

So are East Coast barrier islands, crowned with lavish fanciful beach-front houses. These islands erode in a special way, recently discovered. The low-lying barriers migrate landward, in effect rolling over on themselves. The landward side accretes, the seaward side, houses and all, disappears. A North Carolina island has recently completed such a somersault in less than a century.

The warmer, fuller sea is constantly searching for relief from its new pressure—billions of added gallons with no place to go—and would burst its confines. It pushes into river mouths, the saltwater migrating upstream. It penetrates underground coastal aquifers where fresh water floats on top of salt-, shoving them landward and upward. Existing wells pump from the newly located saltwater layer, to the surprise and dismay of householders expecting a cool fresh drink. Occupants have to discover a new source of fresh water, if they want to continue to live where they are.

The upwardly mobile sea level is a fact of life. With the rise of another inch, it will damage seaside highways, cutting off some of the places these vulnerable roads take you to. The water will inundate docks, airports, bridges, buildings that edge rivers and harbors. It is an ironic footnote that we finally got around to restoring some harbors to what they once were—bustling, fascinating mixtures of commerce and the glamour of seagoing men and ships— just in time to watch the sea drown such places as Boston's Faneuil Hall, New York's South Street Seaport, and San Francisco's Fisherman's Wharf.

The EPA Sea Rise Study details what will happen to Galveston, Texas, which embraces a huge petrochemical industry built on a low flood plain, and Charleston, South Carolina, on the Atlantic, fronted by barrier islands. Cities share many similar problems in the time of a rising sea. One is what will happen to toxic waste storage. Galveston has ten hazardous waste facilities in the path of serious floods; by the year 2075, the rising waters will cover twenty-two more. In Charleston, there are now five on the flood plain; five more will be included when the water rises. Storage tanks and various other containers, not built for a nautical life, will be inundated, corroded, floated, releasing wastes which include carcinogens such as arsenic, benzene, cadmium, and a variety of lethal pesticides.

The terrors of toxic wastes, floating free in an incoming sea, surpass the leaks, spills, and accidents which have plagued the land in the last few years. Had we acted on the knowledge acquired a century ago that the sea rise was upon us, we might have planned these receptacles differently, put them on a mountaintop, or devised a safer disposal strategy. As it is, the failure to look ahead threatens lives.

In other instances, the cost is in money. A seawall, for example, might be underdesigned if there were no information about the future; with such information, it could be built to last out its

112

natural existence. "The value of information," the EPA report says, "would be savings from not having to rebuild the seawall." A building has a life of fifty to one hundred years; a road influences development for even longer. Decisions to build on vulnerable coast land are loaded with losses. Factor in a rising sea and you reroute the road, build temporary or movable structures, or don't build at all, and save millions.

These are more than naive environmentalist predictions. Advice to understand the warming climate and act on it is now beamed to corporate directors. In a recent publication, they are urged to consider the climate change in order to give their companies a competitive edge. Firms in the biomass business should choose plants that are helped to grow faster by CO_2. Since there will be an excess available, such choices will yield higher profits sooner. Conversely, a company that develops a major coastal resort·"may find its investment short-lived . . . and suffer lawsuits for failure to warn buyers of potential risks." The promise of long-range profit by attention to the warming world courts corporate interest.

Money is one reason to start planning for the heat now. Time is another. Most of the new realities will not wait. Planting new forests, for example, has to start soon; preparing soil takes years. Ways to fight infectious diseases from hookworm, mosquitoes, and other carriers that thrive in warm, damp climate need intensive research. To protect the population from the swarm of plagues that flourish in the heat requires decades.

Scientists, environmentalists, commentators of many stripes almost unanimously agree that there is no chance to stop the accumulation of CO_2 in the sky. "A natural reaction to all this is to call for massive reductions in the output of CO_2," says an article in *Amicus*, the journal of the environmentally minded Natural Resources Defense Council. "However, that public policy choice does not exist." In *Foreign Affairs*, among many others, climatologists reach the same conclusion: "Efforts to control fossil fuel use and carbon dioxide emissions on a worldwide basis would face extremely tough political opposition. . . . Agreement to limit fossil fuels seems out of the question for some time to come."

Most opinion makers, like these, say there is nothing that can be done about the warming, if indeed they admit that it is happening. Quoted and requoted, the no-chance-to-stop stance is becoming better established than it deserves. We have not tried and failed. We have not even tried. The global conflict—ocean versus energy—remains unsolved.

If the world cannot agree to stop CO_2 increase in the atmosphere, to stop burning fossil fuels, the entire globe will suffer the warming. When oil runs out, as predicted for the early twenty-first century, if we switch to coal, it will make matters even worse. Coal emits more carbon dioxide than oil for the same amount of energy. But there is no sign that our power-driven society intends to lessen its reliance on energy.

Response to the warming dangers is up to us, each person, each nation. Leadership in this almost unbelievable drama belongs to the U.S., largest user of energy. What can be done?

It is possible to step up the losing battle to fight the change, armoring the shore against waves and storms, turning up the air-conditioner against the increasing heat. Or man can adapt to the warming. The most intelligent adaptation is to try to slow the growth rate of CO_2 by whatever means can be summoned—conservation of energy, alternate energy—to give ourselves time to prepare for the hot world. Exploration of effects on the ocean as it warms and rises is the ultimate requirement. Centuries hence the ocean might save the world by storing all the excess carbon dioxide in its depths. We cannot let it boil away.

8

OCEAN GRAB: MAKING IT LEGAL

The ocean rolled and roared, unruled as it was unex-
plored, until the first years of the seventeenth century. Then Grotius, a young Dutch lawyer, hired to defend an act of piracy, made
a statement. The sea, he said, is free—*Mare liberum*—and the world
agreed. This became the law of the sea. In the eighteenth century,
the law of the sea expanded to give each coastal nation the right to
a 3-mile strip offshore, so that it might better protect itself from
uninvited visitors, be they warriors, pirates, or other intruders.

This generation has created a formal Law of the Sea that be-
stows the world's blessing on nations which would own a piece of
the ocean.

The global Law of the Sea (LOS) Convention is nationalism
in a diving suit, creeping through the waves and along the sea bottom. It is also a great deal more than that. We are lucky, in the
early 1980s, to know with some precision where society stands in
relation to the ocean, how it intends to use it, share it, protect it.
The LOS is a freshly minted statement of intent, created by the
nations in solemn concord. The product of fifteen years of international negotiations, the law was at long last ready for signing in
December, 1982, on the island of Jamaica, BWI. Sixty to seventy
signatures were expected; instead 117 nations signed, twenty-one
abstained, and one—the United States—said no.

A clear reflection of today's man-ocean relation is mirrored in
the LOS proposal. It will formally become international law when

117

ratified by a minimum of sixty nations in the course of the next several years. The U.S. holds its own mirror wherein a trumpeting elephant momentarily obscures the scene.

The new law is said to be the most immense legal undertaking since the Code of Justinian. It codifies contemporary realities. Nations have rights to an Exclusive Economic Zone 200 miles out from their shore, and to their continental shelf, rich in fish and oil. The 3-mile "sovereign" zone can extend from the traditional 3 to 12 miles offshore. "As regards navigation and fishing which were *Mare liberum* concerns," says Professor Louis Henkin of Columbia Law School, who has long been involved in the creation of the new law, "60 percent of the oceans remain free for both and the other 30 to 40 percent are essentially free for navigation."

Dividing this part of the sea was hardly a problem compared to disposing of the treasures of the seabed out under the still free, unowned deep, the mineral-rich manganese nodules. The U.S. and other large industrial nations are developing technology to harvest them and argue, not surprisingly, that the nodules belong to whoever gets them first. Third World nations insist that they are entitled to a share.

The LOS hammered out a Jovian resolution of the conflict. Ironically, as it turns out, harvesting the nodules may be neither as alluring nor necessary as had been thought. The metal-heavy ore pouring out of sea-floor rifts, only just discovered, is more accessible, closer to home and much less of a problem as far as ownership is concerned.

The first LOS conference in 1958 confirmed what the nations wanted, including the desired widening of the continental shelf out to the end of the continental margin. The only thing that was not settled then, or at the second conference in 1960, was the matter of fishing rights, an endlessly debated concern. A third conference, suggested by Ambassador Arvid Pardo of Malta in 1967, finally got under way in 1973, "the most significant single event in the history of law and peaceful cooperation among nations since

118

the creation of the United Nations," according to Ambassador El-liot Richardson, who for some years headed the U.S. Delegation to the LOS Conference. "If the Law of the Sea Conference fails," Lord Ritchie Calder, M.P., observes, "there will be the biggest smash and grab since the European powers carved up Black Africa in 1885. . . ."

LOS is a package deal. A new slice of the sea and a licensed opportunity to mine the deep go hand in hand with dozens of other measures, passage through straits, conduct of scientific research, arbitration to resolve disputes. It required hundreds of representa-tives of many nations to put use of the sea into law, and the fact of this colossal effort, its drama, its internationalism, the actual ex-istence of the law today, often obscures the alarming reflection of reality in its looking glass.

"Today's realism becomes the madness of tomorrow," is the prescient comment of Wolfgang Friedman, respected Columbia University law professor (who was mercilessly shot down by hood-lums on a streetcorner). In his *The Future of the Oceans*, concern for the world attitude toward the sea is paramount. Today that concern is clearly deserved.

Almost every LOS discussion includes an abbreviated litany of the past. It generally hops from Grotius' seventeenth-century freedom-of-the-sea doctrine to the spectacular reversal of that free-dom in the mid-twentieth century when, in 1945, President Tru-man's Proclamations ensured that the natural resources of the shelf around our continent henceforth belonged to the United States. From this juncture, the story takes another hop to November 1967, when Ambassador Pardo appealed to the United Nations, and thence, fifteen years later, to the 1982 signing in Jamaica.

It is a puzzling story. One must wonder why the Dutch doc-trine came to be, why the bold move into the ocean by a brand-new U.S. president, man of the Middle West, why, in fact, the creation of the new Law of the Sea came about. The interstitial tissue reveals more of motive than the milestones.

119

A bright young Dutchman was born in Delft in 1583 to the ancient, noble DeGroot family. Hugo entered Leiden University at age eleven, took his oath as a lawyer at sixteen, and eventually became the foremost scholar, theologian, lawyer, and statesman of his day. At the time, Portugal and Spain had divided the recognized ocean between them by a 1494 papal decree. Portuguese ships were shooting at Dutch trading ships en route to the East Indies, calling them "rovers and trespassers" in seas which the Portuguese claimed to be their own.

The Dutch East Indies Company hired lawyer DeGroot because one of their captains had captured a rich Portuguese galleon in the Straits of Malacca. The lawfulness of this action was challenged in Holland. It was necessary to the defense of piracy to show that the Portuguese pretense of owning this part of the ocean was untenable. For this purpose the lawyer wrote a book, *De Jure Praedae*, signing himself Grotius. Part III is *Mare liberum*, in which the author asserts that peaceful trading is free to all, and so the sea is free, being the property of no one and everyone. A rough translation of his words is startling when compared to our perspective of the ocean: "The vagrant waters of the sea are . . . necessarily free," Grotius writes. "The right of occupation rests upon the fact that most things become exhausted by promiscuous use. But this is not the case with the sea; it can be exhausted neither by navigation nor by fishing, that is to say in neither of the two ways in which it can be used."

There was a flurry of disagreement from across the channel. "The King of Great Britain is the Lord of the Seas flowing about," writes John Selden, lawyer, in 1635, "as an inseparable and perpetual appendant of the British Empire." However, *Mare liberum* was regnant.

The idea of protecting free seas from encroachment had, as yet, no reason to be born. As long as fish and navigation were the sole riches to be derived from the sea, and there was plenty of both to accommodate the world population, *Mare liberum* made sense.

120

In a fast-changing civilization, this comparatively placid state of affairs could not last. Settlements across the sea burgeoned. Soon the U.S.A., even in its infancy, wanted to assert neutrality, keeping itself safe from marauders and out of foreign wars, should that be possible. For this purpose, the statesmen of the time reached for a protective margin around the coast. Secretary of State Jefferson sent a note to the British foreign minister in 1793, making an official American claim for a 3-mile zone into the water at the edge of the continent. "The U.S. has stood for freedom of the seas throughout its existence," a court opinion upholding the claim stated. "The three-mile rule is but a recognition that [it] must be able to protect itself from dangers incident to its location."

There is no partisan on record for keeping the sea whole and unowned. Safety of the new nation was paramount, and there seemed to be no concern about using the sea to secure it. For a while, the 3-mile belt fit what it had been designed for, to keep intruders a cannon shot off American shores while maintaining the desired neutrality and freedom of the rest of the ocean. This very first ownership of a part of the sea appears innocent enough. Surely Thomas Jefferson did not foresee that it would be the start of the ultimate division of the indivisible ocean . . . "the madness of tomorrow."

The next huge step away from *Mare liberum* was taken by none other than President Franklin D. Roosevelt, wanting to protect fish and to garner for the nation the natural riches buried in the continental shelf. President Roosevelt, who liked to call himself alternately "The Old Conservationist" and "a tree farmer," according to the distinguished biographer Joseph P. Lash, was a masterful politician in preparing the takeover of ocean real estate. An accident of timing obscured his efforts; most accounts hardly mention them.

Fishing and navigation were the only ocean values apparent to Grotius. One more—a barrier against attack of the new nation—was added in the eighteenth century. In Roosevelt's era, two additional uses of the sea appeared imperative. Protection of living resources and the harvest of nonliving resources pressed for attention.

Discovery that oil and gas were buried in the Outer Continental Shelf (OCS) had been made and the technology to retrieve them existed. At the turn of the century, oil companies were drilling in a few feet of water off California shores; by mid-century they were ready to probe deeper. California did a thriving business in leasing underwater lands to oil companies, the states, rather than the federal government, being the proprietors of the 3-mile territorial seabed. Therein ensued a tug-of-war. With Harold Ickes, President Roosevelt's secretary of the interior, in charge, the U.S. made a determined effort to wrest control of the 3-mile zone and its newly available riches from the states.

At the same time, "The Old Conservationist" was after a seaward extension of U.S. underwater lands. He was intent on protecting Alaskan salmon and crabs on their way to and from their river spawning grounds. President Roosevelt believed the U.S. should claim the Pacific from the 3-mile limit out to a water depth of 100 fathoms as territorial waters "indispensable to the proper safeguarding of this important food supply of the American people." It could be, he wrote to Sumner Welles, assistant secretary of state, "a national game preserve in which no fishing . . . could be undertaken."

The plan was shelved because of World War II. As these words are written, almost a half-century later, the imminent extinction of Alaskan crabs makes newspaper headlines: "King Crab Fishing Closed Out In Alaska." The story says that one hundred percent of adult females captured in 1983 were barren.

Toward the end of the war, Roosevelt and Ickes designed an ocean policy which claimed for the nation the living and nonliving resources of the OCS, satisfying the two needs they perceived for the sea. The cut into *Mare liberum* was considerable. One commentator puts it at 2.4 million square miles of the earth's crust, an area larger than all of Napoleon's empire. To prepare for this radical move, there had been the ubiquitous study, struggles between the departments of Interior and State, and, finally, a compromise—*two* presidential proclamations. One grabbed the continental shelf; the fishing proclamation asserted the right to conserve, not to grab for oneself. On March 31, 1945, President Roosevelt approved the documents. The State Department insisted that the new idea of management of ocean space which these embodied should be discussed abroad to forestall hostile reactions. A delay ensued.

On April 12th, Roosevelt died. The two proclamations were made the following September by the incumbent president. Thus the landmark "Truman Proclamations."

It is not appropriate here to analyze the Roosevelt-Ickes reasoning in depth. Suffice it to recognize that despite excellent intentions, the soul-shaking reality is that even these renowned statesmen were unable to look ahead and see where this revolutionary action would lead.

A fascinating little-known byplay, Professor Henkin tells us, is that in the Nixon era, the U.S. reversed direction. It started out resisting the coastal grab, even favored keeping a narrow continental shelf, perhaps because the Pentagon feared wide coastal control generally. "Then the oil companies won their push for a wide continental shelf; U.S. domestic fishing interests beat out our 'distant-fishing' interests, pressing for a wide fishing zone, and hence accepting a wide fishing zone for all other states." The Pentagon, he says, was then persuaded and pressured to go along. Thus is ocean real estate dispensed.

The Roosevelt-Ickes-Truman proclamation of possessible ocean was the music of a pied piper. Chile, Peru, and Ecuador immediately followed the U.S. lead, claiming zones 200 miles out from their coasts. Soon a large collection of nations lined up behind the idea. "It was generally accepted in thirteen years," Friedman comments, "while such new law generally takes decades if not centuries to become general practice." By the late 1970s, it had caught on around the world. Over 100 nations claimed territorial seas ranging from 12 to 200 miles. It is staggering to realize that the total of all these seas is an area greater than the earth's whole land-mass.

Together the nations of the world were caught in an international tangle. The skein of sea relationships was no longer simple and free. Problems over passage through straits, freedom of navigation, of marine research, of overflight, and dozens of other such issues highlighted the impossibility of sharing ocean use according to the old Grotius doctrine in the new wet real estate era. Nations exploding with growth coveted resources under the waves just as the U.S. had. They wanted to own part of the sea and at the same time to move freely through it. Without international agreement, there was chaos.

Fights over fish proliferated. Floating refrigerated factories now enabled the big nations to go fishing around the world, intruding on the take of small developing nations which needed what their own waters could provide. The scramble not only pitted big against small, but north against south, neighbor against neighbor. The U.S. established a 200-mile exclusive fishing zone, chased Russian trawlers which strayed within its limits. Peru, with a 200-mile maritime zone, including water column and seabed, arrested U.S. tuna boats "trespassing" in its territory. Iceland shot at British codfishers.

Boundary clashes exploded everywhere. In the Arctic Ocean, Norwegian sailors boarded half a dozen Danish fishing trawlers, warning the Danes to leave. The waters are claimed by both countries, being where their 200-mile economic zones overlap. Such incidents sprang up between Iceland and Great Britain, Greece and Turkey, Spain and Portugal, virtually everywhere in the seven seas.

The new importance of the deep-sea floor proved an even more compelling need for some sort of law and order to extend *Mare liberum*. Beyond any territorial claims are an estimated 1.5 trillion

124

tons of manganese nodules lying in incredible profusion some 3 miles down in the ocean deep. The nodules, resembling black potatoes, contain nickel, copper, cobalt, and, of course, manganese, all valuable in industrial processes. They are mostly in the South Pacific and the Indian Ocean, with some scattered elsewhere on the seabed, discovered there by the nineteenth-century *Challenger* explorations. At that time there was no inkling of what they were worth or how they might be harvested.

In the early '80s, Marne Dubs, then at the Kennecott Copper Corporation, in charge of its ocean resources division, mentioned to a visitor that the black potatoes are "the most significant untapped source of mineral raw materials known to the world . . . of such burning importance that (by 1978) more than two hundred million dollars has been spent by industry on ocean mining technology. The resource," Dubs said, "is truly immense, easily doubling the world resources base, and can serve as a major mineral supply long into the future."

To whom does it belong?

Claims to the seabed treasure, more than any other conflict, might have been the issue that stirred Malta's U.N. Ambassador to call for a law for the sea. "The dark oceans were the womb of life," Pardo said. "Man's penetration of the deep could mark the beginning of the end for man (or) a prosperous future for all peoples." Pardo characterized the seabed resources as "the common heritage of mankind," an idea which became a magnet for contention in drafting the Law of the Sea.

The common heritage concept has a background, often overlooked. Commons have been known on land throughout history. The urge to overuse the land inspires a comment on man's essential nature in Garret Hardin's *The Tragedy of the Commons*. In brief, the tragedy Hardin describes is villagers' use of common grazing lands. Because these lands were both common to all and free, each man tried to outdo the next in his use of them. Neighbor raced his

125

flocks against neighbor. Eventually, the commons, overgrazed, were useless to all. True, those were land commons but the idea can be equally applied to the sea.

Bernardo Zuleta, under secretary general of the United Nations, who died in the winter of '83, had vigorously put down the myth that the common heritage concept had been invented during one U.N. session. "Any serious student of international law knows that the idea was suggested before the turn of the century by a famous French publicist, Monsieur de Lapradelle," Zuleta said, "surfaced again many years later in a speech by Prince Wan Waithayakon of Thailand . . . and became a major point of U.S. policy in 1966 in a speech by President Johnson." Johnson said, "Under no circumstance, we believe, must we ever allow the prospects of rich harvest and mineral wealth to create a new form of colonial competition among the maritime nations. We must insure that the deep seas and the ocean bottoms are, and remain, the legacy of all human beings." President Nixon made a similar proposal to the United Nations. He suggested that ". . . all nations adopt as soon as possible a treaty under which they would renounce all national claims over the natural resources of the seabed beyond (a depth of 200 meters) and would agree to regard these resources as the common heritage of mankind." Many nations were surprised that the United States supported the proposal so strongly at the presidential level.

Once the Third Conference began, there were three committees for drafting the LOS. Maritime law was the province of Committee Two under Ambassador Aquilar of Venezuela. Pollution and scientific research matters were the business of Committee Three led by Ambassador Yankov of Bulgaria. But it was Committee One, concerned with the seabed, that stirred the deepest emotions, took the most time, and produced a completely original solution.

The seabed was more than just an issue, William Wertenbaker says in his detailed description of the negotiations in *The New*

Yorker. "It was a vision . . . and it afforded a chance to create a cooperative world project." As will be seen, this vision became crystal clear in the LOS mirror, a merciless reflection of the limits of contemporary compassion of man for man.

A visit to Committee One in session was a drama of impassioned speeches, knots of conferring members, messengers on the move. On the dais, resplendent in his pale-blue flowing native robes, a gold-encrusted black hat, and a large cigar, is Paul Engo, lawyer and diplomat from Cameroon, who has chaired the Committee since 1974 and is known in U.N. circles as The King. "We owe it to peace and world freedom to resolve this issue," Engo tells a visitor, "and being an eternal optimist I think we will." Engo says that his distinctive dress is strictly protective: "There are lots of people around who would like to strangle me with a tie. So I wear this. No tie."

Engo wrestles with putting the common heritage of mankind into practice, a so-far untried, philosophical, economic, and practical exercise. The big industrial nations have the technology to mine the deep seabed. One system, for example, is to suck up the nodules on the deep-sea floor with a giant vacuum cleaner and pump them through a pipe to the dredge ship 3 miles up on the surface; another is an endless chain of buckets which would scoop up the treasure and dump it into the waiting ship. Although it sounds simple enough, costs are enormous, so much so that most big mineral companies, in preparation, have organized into consortia to share the burden.

Third World nations were determined that disposition of the deep-sea riches should in fact be the common heritage of mankind, themselves included. "They wanted all the economic benefits and the exclusive rights to mining," Professor Louis Henkin says, "apparently dreaming of great wealth that would transform the world economic system and eliminate the chasm between rich and poor." The Third World's solid bloc, organized into the Group of 77, threatened independent mining with round-the-world har-

127

rassment. By making a mining site insecure, the bloc could discourage the investment of the billion or more dollars necessary for a mine.

There was fierce determination on both sides and finally, in 1980, a unique compromise was reached. It was a triumph for the Cameroon diplomat, with an assist to break a deadlock from then secretary of state, Henry Kissinger. Under a new International Seabed Authority, any national enterprise, or private enterprise, organized into an international consortia, could gain half the mining sites and the Authority's corporate arm, the *Enterprise*, would have the other half. In exchange for the privilege of mining, industrialized countries would underwrite *Enterprise* and sell it the necessary technology.

U.S. mining and oil interests were impatient, ready to mine. Besides Kennecott, since purchased by Sohio, there was U.S. Steel, Lockheed, Standard Oil, and others which pressed hard for U.S. legislation in 1980—the Deep Seabed Hard Mineral Resources Act. It allows the U.S. to grant licenses to prospective miners, although actual mining cannot start until 1988 to give *Enterprise* a chance to get under way. West Germany and other countries followed suit to promote a flow of funds for the billion-dollar deep-sea adventure.

Seabed mining and its many international issues occupied center stage for a considerable portion of the lengthy LOS discussions. So intense was the argument that several more significant, if less flamboyant questions were not much noticed.

The deep seabed (benthos) is one of the least well-understood areas of the globe, until recently being out of man's reach. Scientists raise dozens of queries about disturbance of the cold, quiet deep by sweeping or vacuuming. In this ecosystem, running on slow ocean time, disruptions take many centuries to recover. A minute example is two hardworking benthic dwellers which make the nodules available in the first instance. Without these two little animals, the slow-growing nodules—they put on between 1 and

128

200 millimeters every million years—would be invisible, buried in the sediment that rains unceasingly from the sea surface. It has recently been discovered that one tiny species keeps busy eating newly arrived sediment off the tops of the nodules and another, for its own unfathomable reasons, moves sediment from sea floor down several centimeters below the nodule. To date their separate activities have kept the black potatoes on the surface of the deep seabed.

If scooped up or vacuumed away, these creatures could take more than 1,000 years to return to present levels, an investigator says. Other marine inhabitants too might be just as severely diminished by the mining and transporting of the nodules through the water column. Harm to species which live where the clock moves in permanent slow motion confronts us with the possibility of eons of damage to the ocean design.

Why the rush to harvest nodules in this stage of ignorance of the effect? The four metals—manganese, copper, cobalt, and nickel—are all necessary to industry, but none is in short supply in 1984 nor expected to be. The U.S. is the world's largest producer of copper, Dubs says, and has "extensive deposits" of the red metal. The other three minerals are imported from reliable sources, most authorities agree.

The U.S. has enough minerals for now. But it would preserve its right to mine the seabed. Clifton Curtis, LOS expert and representative for many environmental groups in the LOS negotiations, says the U.S. is in pursuit of "the most ancient of corporate goals: to corner the market." Mining the nodules is considered a futuristic activity. Minerals, a Conservation Foundation study says, have become a "hot economic item." In line with all this, President Reagan has announced a $10 billion plan to buy and stockpile strategic minerals for U.S. defense.

The LOS treaty was adopted in April, 1982. In July, President Reagan announced that the U.S. would not sign. Our nation had spent years, under three administrations, cooperating with, if not leading, the states of the world to fashion a law for the sea,

129

and had won more compromises than any other state. The Reagan administration now departed the scene for its own particular reasons with, it must be assumed, its own powerful backing.

The President, Wertenbaker says, is reported to have explained, somewhat informally, to the Cabinet at a meeting where the decision was made: "We're policed and patrolled on land and there is so much regulation that I kind of thought that when you go out on the high seas you can do as you want." To do what you want in this instance is to ignore the bothersome common heritage idea, and its insistence on sharing the wealth. "The deep seabed mining part of the convention does not meet United States objectives," according to Reagan's formal statement. It was expanded on by Ambassador James Malone, head of the U.S. delegation: "Put directly—the principal objection was that the political, economic, and ideological assumptions which underlie the treaty are essentially antithetical to American values in these areas."

The seabed as "a vision of a cooperative world project" did not catch the imagination of the Reagan administration; it did not move such as U.S. Steel, or Secretary of State Haig, to change their views. "If we want the resources, then we should just go and get them," Haig said. U.S. Steel agreed.

With a little luck, the Reagan administration might have saved itself the uncomplimentary labels its common heritage views accumulated abroad and at home. In the 1970s, while LOS committees searched for accord, scientists were diverted from fascination with nodules to a newly discovered source of seabed minerals in shallower, near-shore waters. Steaming out of rifts in the ocean floor at 450°C, mineral-rich material sizzles to a halt on meeting 2°C bottom water, bonds itself to sulfides, and quickly solidifies. The result is polymetallic sulfides.

This ore grows a foot or more a year, in contrast to nodules, which add an inch in a million years. It includes a wide assortment of minerals—copper, zinc, silver, and manganese. Copper, one of the most desirable, can comprise 30 percent of the sulfide, dwarfing the 1 percent in nodules. Cecily Murphy, a Law of the Sea expert, contrasting the two mineral sources, says that an 8-foot cube of sulfides weighs a ton while the equivalent minerals in nodules, far heavier, could cover acres of the ocean bottom. The sulfides are thought to be easier and cheaper to mine, and inch for inch vastly more valuable.

In the autumn of 1981, NOAA scientists under Alexander Malahoff, located "the most massive sulfide deposit ever found" on the Galapagos Rift, where children and sea lions might swim on the surface, some 500 miles off Peru's coast. The copper alone, they claimed, may be worth $2 billion. A year later, Dr. Peter Rona of NOAA, heading a team of scientists from the Woods Hole Oceanographic Institution, made a great find on the bottom of the Atlantic, 1,800 miles east of Miami. There in 10,000 feet of water along the wall of an underwater mountain range, were 2 miles of deposits, "black, orange and green layers of material rich in manganese and iron," the *New York Times* reports. "It's just a world of manganese down there," Dr. Rona said. The explorers, using the Woods Hole submersible research vessel *Alvin*, managed to break off pieces of the sulfide with *Alvin*'s mechanical arm. At the Juan de Fuca Ridge off Oregon and Washington, scientists from the U.S. Geological Survey and the University of Washington searched for the sulfides with a sled carrying two cameras in a steel tube cage, Randolph Koski, scientist, reports. Photographs at eleven stations showed fresh glossy basalt; at the twelfth, there was a clear picture of massive amounts of metal sulfide.

"Hot spots" for polymetalic sulfides range from the Red Sea to the Fiji Islands. Again, the world wonders whom such riches belong to. The U.S., rubbing its collective hands, perceives that some of the ore—in the Gorda Rift and the Juan De Fuca Rift— is within 200 miles of our shores and comparatively easy to reach. Again, it figures a way to corner this new abundant mineral supply. With no further ado, disregarding the effect on the very start of LOS proceedings, the U.S. establishes a 200-mile Exclusive

131

Economic Zone (EEZ) and gives itself, among other assets, the right to start mining.

The U.S. would forget that LOS is a package deal and decides to choose among the LOS rights and responsibilities those that it likes and call them "customary ocean law." James Malone, then a State Department official and special representative of the president to the Law of the Sea Conference, explains, in response to a query from this writer. His letter of October 19, 1983 says in part:

> The United States finds unacceptable certain parts of the Convention related to deep seabed mining and therefore has refused to sign the LOS Convention. However, since the U.S. recognizes much of the balance of the Convention as customary international law, including the establishment of EEZ's, the President promulgated the establishment of a U.S. EEZ.

Criticism of unilateral U.S. action will be even angrier when it is discovered that the U.S. intends to use its EEZ for dumping toxic wastes in bulk, thus further polluting the world's waters, and is again actively considering the ocean as a disposal medium for radioactive wastes. In 1983, this nation, operating outside of international law, makes its own decisions.

Since the LOS was a gleam in Pardo's eye, the U.S. participated actively in negotiations. One president after another announced the nation's belief in oceangoing law and order and the common heritage of mankind. The commitment was powerful; it appeared without question that the U.S. was negotiating in good faith. It moved slowly but steadily with the world's many nations toward accord, the work of more than a decade.

Suddenly, without notice, President Reagan reversed the U.S. position, withdrew from LOS. His lack of respect for our nation's intentions, hammered out over so many years, shocked participants preparing to sign the treaty. Reasons for the reversal were superficially explained, hardly challenged.

132

The nation was apathetic. There was no outcry, no demand for public debate, no insistence, as there was in the case of firing former Secretary of Interior Watt, that Reagan's judgment measure up to the nation's standards. President Reagan did not see to it that the electorate understood that he was turning his back on the family of nations. He just did it.

Then, without fanfare, the Reagan administration tried to undercut the LOS. In November, 1982, just before the December signing, it sent envoy Donald Rumsfeld to West European nations and to Japan to try to persuade them to join the U.S. defection. The U.S. proclaimed its EEZ just one week before meetings to get LOS under way began. This takeover of 1.4 billion acres of ocean space could stimulate other nations to make nontreaty sea grabs, just as the Truman Proclamations set off the first wave of anarchy almost forty years ago.

Whether history will repeat itself is still to be seen. Professor Henkin and other scholars agree that the LOS proposal may be the best we can get just now. "It should be put into effect as soon as possible," Henkin says. "And it is in the United States' interest to adhere to it promptly. The convention will bring order, reasonable certainty as to what to expect, confidence, reliability. Anarchy jeopardizes our every national interest."

In the long progression of ocean use, the Law of the Sea is no surprise. The limited blue expanse visible to early mariners allowed a sea free to all. There was plenty of room to sail across the waves, trading, exploring, and plenty of fish to feed the global population. With the advent of ownership—the 3-mile protective zone—the world went into the ocean real estate business, if in a modest way. Business was so profitable that competition for resources, transportation, rights of all sorts, required that we recognize ocean ownership and make it legal. The idea of sharing sea-floor riches gives the endeavor something of a soul, a late twentieth-century mark of progress, a subtheme in the dominant triumphal march of the national ocean grab.

The nations have labored hard and brought forth a law that divides the sea, legalizing the ocean grab, and stating that each nation shall make its own decisions about its own ocean property, now a sizable proportion of the whole. Such anarchy does not suit the sea. It is too late for the pirate to ruthlessly chase down his pieces of eight. Dividing the indivisible ocean will necessarily lead to irreversible disaster.

But the long struggle for a law to meet contemporary requirements has its value. The Law of the Sea is a step toward international accord on matters marine. It is a beginning, however flawed, of world law for the world ocean. From this base the world can take the next step and legislate ocean survival.

9

TRYING TO MANAGE

The United States has acquired a splendid expanse of ocean real estate that contains copious resources and an extraordinary amount of space for our discards. But the rapture of ownership of this magnificent empire escapes us. As we use it, it responds with unanticipated turmoil. Rapture has a price. The price is to decide what we want to use the ocean for.

One must wonder what the nation's intentions are. The title of the new empire is suggestive—the Exclusive Economic Zone— and many colloquies now take place to map its future. Nothing has yet been formalized into law to legislate the fate of these rich rolling waters. There is still time to consider.

In the Victorian era, British aristocracy made a drawing room version of such a decision on a microscopic scale. For a few decades in mid-nineteenth century, ornamental aquaria decorated Mayfair conservatories. In them were marvelously fanciful forms of goldfish, bred over centuries; a specialist describes the Celestial, "its bulging eyes gazing forever upward." Other marine animals shared the glass home, mollusks, periwinkles and plants, collected from the coast. The fancier the fish, the more graceful the plants and the more elaborate the container, the more prestigious was the aquarium and its owner. It was a fad, a bit of preciousness to add to the glitter of the times.

The ornate vessel was effete, amusing, but it also gave London's upper crust a view of an entire working ecosystem. From it,

137

its beholders could learn, relatively painlessly, the principles of life in the sea.

The aquarium's immediate ancestor was the fishbowl. On the continent and in England, people of the time kept goldfish and various other sea dwellers in glass containers, just as children do today, feeding the fish and changing the water each day to provide oxygen. Anne Thynne, a London lady enchanted with stony corals, brought them back from the Devonshire coast, kept them in jars of water which her maid poured back and forth every morning in front of an open window. In Scotland, Sir John Graham Dalyell, 6th Baronet of Binns, had his porter bring several gallons of seawater three times a week, keeping his specimens alive for years, especially a sea anemone named "Granny," which survived for sixty years, the story goes, "long outliving Sir John and several others to whom it was passed on."

Meanwhile, the chemical conception of nature was being enthusiastically explored by the great naturalists and chemists of the era. The circle of organic life—photosynthesis—was firmly established. London chemists used the new knowledge in aquaria with various combinations of seaweed, snails (to clean up the debris), pebbles, and fish. Too many fish or too much greenery, and the system drooped. The owner's only responsibility was to keep the community in balance. When in equilibrium, the water did not need to be changed for years; the sole requirement was daily food for fish. Otherwise, like the orderly ecosystem it was, it worked independently of man.

Soon enough, aquaria became great public shows, crammed with specimens of all kinds without much thought to equilibrium. The ecosystem required artificial supports to keep functioning. The Victorians gave up as "too troublesome" the admirably simple copy of nature which adorned their homes.

The message of how the ocean works, even the simple view of it in a glass box with minimum components, resounds over more than a hundred years and across the sea. With all that has happened to the ocean in the intervening century, it can never achieve pre-twentieth-century purity again. We have intruded into the sea in dozens of ways, taking our chances that the big ocean will keep functioning as it always has.

In the ocean of the 1980s, bluefish streak up the Atlantic coast suffused with a potent toxic. A nursing mother who dines on a big blue gives her baby many times more poison in its blood than she herself absorbs. The baby is more likely to become seriously ill with cancer or other diseases than the mother and the multitude who eat the delectable fish. The danger for all is so grave that in 1983, four Northeast coastal states issued warnings to their citizens about eating blues. The situation can only worsen. Despite scientific urging, the U.S. Food and Drug Administration has not raised the "safe" tolerance level of this toxic. The dollar loss that would be incurred was the deciding factor. The U.S. Environmental Protection agency, which banned further manufacture of the toxic in the 1970s, recently authorized continuing use of the millions of pounds that now exist. The blues will, no doubt, continue to run with it.

The U.S.A. acquired its new billions of ocean acres without spending a dime. Now we have to decide whether we want to manage the sea so that it comes close to its natural balance once again, a condition wherein bluefish do not carry poison to suckling infants. If this is the choice, President Reagan's wish for freedom in the sea must give way to wisdom which will bring about the serene state of ocean equilibrium. Otherwise the new U.S. territory will be worth exactly what we paid for it. Worse still, it will threaten our survival.

There are countless ocean systems to be managed and myriad government tiers which take a hand in their control. On the national level alone, there are departments for fisheries, oil, pollution, floods; there is the Environmental Protection Agency, the Food and Drug Administration, the Departments of Interior, Commerce, and State, the Coast Guard, the National Oceanic and Atmospheric Administration and dozens more which oversee the sea.

States have their own hierarchy for the 3-mile zone under their jurisdiction; so do cities.

So far, the agencies of government have been eminently unsuccessful in managing the sea. Goals are unknown, responsibilities are undefined, money is scarce, and the whole operation is so complex that it is almost impossible to tell who should be doing what. I tried to unravel the confusion which reigns over the New York Bight but had to give up. By reliable count, an incredible 400 local, state, and federal agencies are involved in management of this busiest, filthiest stretch of ocean in the world.

The heart of ocean management is to keep marine life alive and healthy. If we fail to do this, the rest will not matter much. Managing people in the cause of fish, and fish for themselves, is urgently needed for our newly acquired real estate and is the backbone of the art of ocean management.

The fish business dominates New Bedford, Massachusetts, the richest fishing town on the East Coast. Fishing accounts for between a quarter and a third of the total income in town. In 1982, the yield was $84.6 million. "If there were no fishing then there would be no New Bedford," Brian Lawler, mayor, tells a visitor. "It would be just another has-been industrial town." He omits part of the picture, an essential part. In the '30s, industrial-minded town fathers went after an electrical manufacturing business to move to New Bedford, "diversifying the industrial base," the Chamber of Commerce *Yearbook* says.

The reach for growth was normal enough. But as it happened, it created a disaster for the town, for fish, fishermen, and fish eaters from which, quite possibly, none may ever recover. There may be no solution to the ensuing New Bedford tragedy.

Fishermen would not want anything dire to happen to what Herman Melville described as "the dearest place to live in, in all New England." That was in the good old whaling days when Greater New Bedford built and launched more than 400 whalers, taking the proud crown away from Nantucket which, because of a silting

140

harbor, was reduced to a mere forty-one whaling ships. In those days whaling was the center of the town's existence. Now it is fish. Whether New Bedford can manage its waters so that the multitude of fish continue to live in that ecosystem is a melodrama playing out before us at this precise moment.

In the early 1980s, life is good to the captains, boat owners, and fishermen of New Bedford. The fleet, grown since the Magnuson Act chased foreign fishermen away, is valued at more than $80 million, some boats upgraded from wood to steel, some new. There are one hundred and twenty-five draggers—for groundfish like haddock, cod, flounder—and fifty-five scalloping boats. New Bedford's wide, deep harbor, which protected whalers, is helpful to the fishing boats. So is the Dike, a 3-mile barrier across the harbor mouth which can be closed in case of a bad storm. It is a marine version of the legendary barn door, having been built after the 1938 hurricane which destroyed much of the town's fishing fleet.

Sometimes owners are captains of their boats, sometimes absentee. One scalloping boat, the *Huntress*, cost $1.2 million and its Norwegian owners, father and son, captain it themselves. They make money, as does their crew, which is supported by a strong union and a co-op which provides low-cost fuel, ice, and food. The financial arrangements are not unusual among the 1,500 fishermen in town. When visited in port, the *Huntress* had been out for eight days, brought back 7,000 pounds of scallops which sold at a record $6.55 a pound for a total of $45,750. The union takes 5 percent off the top, the owner takes 35 percent, from which he pays various fixed expenses, and the crew splits the rest; they pay for food, fuel, ice. The crew's other expenses—rubber boots, oilskins and shucking knives—are minimal. Fishermen work long hours, and clear an average of $50,000 a year.

Currently, a sense of success pervades New Bedford. Fishing is profitable. The sleepy streets and quiet offices suggest that the docks and the auction where fish gets sold are where the action is. At eight in the morning, in the small red-brick auction house, boat captains sell their catch in a wildly confusing competitive auction between many boats and maybe a dozen products—fish of different species, size, and weight. Buyers, representing fish processors, bid, incomprehensibly to a visitor, until the last second before a bell ends the quarter-hour competition. The scallop auction an hour before is quieter, there being fewer boats and one product.

Once sold, the fish is weighed and checked for quality on the wharf. Disagreement is not unusual, fights not uncommon. The fish may look crushed, undersized, not fresh. Eventually, bargains are struck and the fish departs by boat or truck to one of the town's ten major processors or fifteen smaller ones. Some are buyers just for a few restaurants. One buys only the "top of the hold" (fish caught no more than two or three days earlier) for exclusive restaurants. After processing, the fish is on its way. You might eat it within the week.

On a summer evening the harbor is bursting with boats, brightly painted hulls giving the disorderd flotilla a pleasing gaiety. The fishing boats tie up at the docks, end to end, heavy chains and metal mats in piles on the decks, stout masts and superstructure for dredges dark against the sky. Strollers on the dock in the sunset find the scene irresistible photographic material.

A closer look reveals that New Bedford is not the fishing paradise it may appear in tourist snapshots and chamber of commerce statistics. The ecosystem of its Acushnet River, the estuary, harbor, and bay beyond is out of sync. Something is very wrong in the waters off the old fishing town on Buzzards Bay. Fishermen do not comment on the unseen threat. What they do worry about is an oil spill in their fishing grounds. They know the terrible results of oil on marine life on the Brittany coast, in the Gulf, and elsewhere, and remember the close call off their own shores in the '70s when the wind changed just in time, sending the oil out to sea. So far, oil is their major concern, and no one advises them otherwise.

Although the fleet does well, it is keeping up its total by taking the fish that used to be caught by the foreign fleets in addition to its usual catch. Many believe that the years of foreign fishing set back fish production. Jim Costakes of the Seafood Producers Association represents all New Bedford fishing boat owners on every level of government, lobbies, goes to regional meetings, serves on the management council. He resents the foreign fishing: "They pulse-fished. When one vessel found a school, a hundred others would join it and fish out the school, clean it out. The resources haven't recovered yet," he says. Costakes thinks management "for a consistent fishery" is essential.

The goal sounds fine and upstanding but its meaning is vague. Without concise goals, it is difficult for a plan to succeed. Fisheries are managed by one of the eight regional councils around the nation which operate under NOAA's National Marine Fisheries Service. Before the Magnuson Act of 1976 the states were in charge; the law designated government councils to oversee fisheries and manage fish. "The U.S. had very little formal and practical management experience prior to the mid-1970s," Spencer Apollonio, first director of the New England Council, says. For example, if the goal is to accumulate as much protein as quickly and cheaply as possible, "often-condemned pulse-fishing is a perfectly legitimate management technique," Apollonio says.

This is short-term management. In today's world, marine life is too fragile to produce an emergency dose of protein and not suffer from that sudden swipe for years. It is the long-term health and welfare of life in the sea that counts.

Fish management generally deals with the presence or absence of one species at a time, about all that managers can manage as they undertake this new experience. Apollonio recalls that the New England Council instituted a quota to rescue haddock which was presumed on the verge of collapse. In six months the fishermen had met the quota for the entire year. Then cod fishing had to be outlawed because haddock are unavoidably caught with cod. This being untenable to the fishermen, the Council made quarterly catch quotas to spread income throughout the year. This did not work either. Small-boat fishermen argued that these quotas discriminated against them. The large boats would take the quota first. Meanwhile haddock catches went unreported. Fish were sold off boats at night or secretly landed at a second port.

Finally the U.S. secretary of commerce scrapped the whole groundfish management effort, closed the haddock spawning area to fishermen, and had it patrolled by Coast Guard boats during the fish's spawning time from March to May.

The original objective was "purely biological," Apollonio says. Then it had to be modified because of political, economic, and social pressures. Pretty soon the Council was uncertain of its own purpose and, in its internal wavering, had no way to measure its success or failure with haddock.

Out on the scallop beds of Georges Bank, productivity dropped about 20 percent from 1982 to 1983, the National Marine Fisheries Service (NMFS) says, following a trend that had started a few years before. New Bedford initiated the sea scallop market in the '60s, raking the fluted bivalves from the Bank, calling itself the Scallop Capital of the World. The fleet was joined by Canada which sent seventy-five government-subsidized boats out scalloping nearby. By 1979, the need for management was clear. In 1982, the catch of the U.S. and of Canada was the lowest in years.

No one knows what happened. It is a long reach to believe the falloff is just a scallop cycle. Maybe the Scallop Capital over-fishes. Maybe the trouble has to do with fish interrelations. An NMFS manager suggests that the scallop decline could be because cod are coming back and enjoy eating baby scallops. Robert Howarth says that in years to come the waters will be loaded with too much oil and other toxics for scallops to manage, although this is probably not yet the problem.

The Council finally agreed on a plan, effective May, 1982, requiring scallopers to take only the bigger scallops, preserving the smaller ones for reproductive activity, which might bring back the scallops. Costakes is pleased to have put enough flexibility in the plan so that changes can be made quickly, locally, "without having to wind their way through the Department of Commerce." Washington's expertise on Georges Bank scallops seems questionable. Fisherman resent the control; they lose money on it, are not used to planning, would let the future take care of itself.

Commercial fishermen are going out of business, infuriated. They vent rage in the wrong direction. Something other than managers has brought about the need for control.

Scallops on Georges Bank are part of a system, an echo from the Victorian aquaria. Basic scientific information is needed to make sense of the interaction in offshore waters, to decide, in the case of scallops, whether the baby scallops are being devoured, not being born, or not growing up, to pinpoint the trouble and try to remedy it. The Council is challenged.

Surprisingly, scientific knowledge which might provide a base for decisions is less than dominant in Council debates. The government recognizes the need for science and requires a committee of scientists for each regional council. Here are typical comments from committee members:

> I do not think we have as great an impact upon Council decisions as we should have. This is partially because we meet on the average only about one day in two months . . . for three or four hours.   Professor of Marine Resources
> in a nearby university.

> We have never had enough information on which to base fishery management decisions. . . . Getting enough information would be cost prohibitive. A rather modest increase in funding would result in substantial improvement in data.
> Chief, State Bureau of Marine Fisheries,
> Department of Environmental Protection

> The Council members are not really interested in the biological information. The Scientist helps the Staff prepare the plans, but

he/she does not help in the decision by the Council member.
The Council is a political body . . . and acts as such.

> Chief staff biologist
> in a marine laboratory

Almost everyone commented on the volunteer aspect of work for the councils, taking time away from jobs or leisure time. "There might be some merit in paying scientists for their service . . . so they might spend more time on council matters," one said.

Asking scientists to volunteer their expertise turns out to be a universal problem, at least in ocean matters, and a shocking exhibition of our culture's disrespect for facts about the sea. The burden of finding out what we are doing to the seas before we do it belongs to the government. We must see to it that our government elevates science to the high place where it belongs and pays its practitioners accordingly. Bureaucracies, the councils included, need every bit of information they can get to manage the tempestuous new problems.

One such problem is born of polychlorinated biphenyls, PCBs. "PCBs should be regarded as carcinogenic to humans," the International Agency for Research on Cancer, part of the World Health Organization, says. (The largest case of human PCB poisoning was in Yusho, Japan, where effects were devastating.) PCBs are what the bluefish run with.

When New Bedford's town fathers of the 1930s looked for industry to broaden the economic base, there were deserted cotton mills on the banks of the Acushnet, which empties into the estuary and harbor. For half a century, a thriving cotton business, part of New England's seminal interest, flourished on the Acushnet, then perished with the Depression. New Bedford's industrialists congratulated themselves when the Aerovax Company from Brooklyn and Cornell Dubilier Electronics agreed to move into the empty mills. Both companies manufactured an electronic part called a capacitor. These capacitors required PCB.

The companies used about 1 million pounds of PCB a year. In peak years in the '70s the amount was closer to 2 million pounds.

Some of the PCB waste was dumped directly into the river and estuary, some into New Bedford's municipal waste-water system. As a result, PCB saturates the sediments of the 985-acre harbor, reaching an astronomical 100,000 ppm, a matter carefully documented in *PCB Pollution in the New Bedford, Massachusetts Area* by Grant Weaver, environmental engineer. The contamination spreads out to Buzzards Bay sediments. "Thousands of acres have been closed to harvesting shellfish, finfish and lobsters because of PCB pollution," Weaver says. Waste from the plants also crowd landfills around town; some tainted oil is used on roads. It's a PCB world in New Bedford.

The PCB in New Bedford's harbor is not about to voluntarily go away. Its low solubility and chemical stability, qualities that make it desirable in industry, make it stubbornly persistent in the environment. After thirty years of study of its effects by scientists, the government stopped its manufacture in 1977. By then 1.4 billion pounds of the compound had been added to the world, a robust fraction of which is on the bottom of the river, estuary, and harbor of New England's richest fishing town.

Management of such disaster has yet to be invented. For New Bedford, as for the Hudson River, Chesapeake Bay, and elsewhere, reaction rather than action dominates, improvised for the occasion. There is no plan, no buttons to push. Even the discovery that PCBs are at large in New Bedford waters was an accident. A Woods Hole scientist, measuring the amounts of oil in harbor sediments in 1974, found PCB in huge proportions. Massachusetts Audubon and the New England Aquarium, private institutions studying for their own special purposes, measured the PCBs. By 1976, a clutch of federal, state, and local agencies were also measuring PCBs in New Bedford waters and out in the bay. The shortage of scientific information and advice in the Council, which, strangely enough, sits on the sidelines in *l'affaire* PCB, was compensated for by these scientists, including a Woods Hole team headed by John Farrington.

"We learned very quickly that it was not realistic or effective to interact with only one level of government," Farrington says in his detailed report. "No mechanism exists to guarantee communication between government entities. . . ." During the discovery process, an ad hoc committee of state and local officials, town leaders, and scientists was assembled to discuss the data and decide what to do. Members were cautious. State officials shied away from the publicity. Local elected officials tried to downplay the PCB contamination problem so as not to alarm the public, discourage tourists and new industry.

The town fathers' ostrichlike behavior demonstrates how unprepared they, like the fishermen, are for the new realities which threaten the town's well-seasoned hope for growth. "The water is a way of life in the New Bedford area," the Chamber of Commerce 1982 *Yearbook* says. "The broad beaches offer sunbathing, swimming and water sports . . . smaller groundfish can be caught from piers and beaches. Digging for clams is a favorite area pastime. . . ." You might not expect the Chamber of Commerce to warn visitors of deadly pollution in fish and shellfish, but one is surprised that it would put itself in such a compromising position in print.

It is even more surprising that an important state official pressures the Department of Public Health to reopen the outer harbor to lobstering. "Lobsters test between 2 ppm and 5 ppm," the official tells an interviewer. "And most people don't eat lobster on a regular basis."

"No one has ever died of PCBs," Costakes, loyal fish business representative, says with assurance. He does not say how he knows. A half-century ago, the world would have shared his confidence. No one then imagined the incipient test-tube terrors.

The witch's brew that turned into PCB was first mixed by the Swann Chemical Company in 1929 in response to industry's needs for an electric insulator that would keep cool and be highly fire-resistant. No permit was needed to bring a new substance into the world, and PCBs turned out to be widely useful, at one time were

148

converted into carbonless carbon paper, printer's ink, floor tiles . . . and food packaging materials. Monsanto bought Swann. Neither company seems to have had any notion of the product's toxicity and potential for harm to the marine environment, Larry O'Neill, a Monsanto spokesman and PCB specialist, says. It was not until 1966 that the Swedish investigator Soren Jensen, looking for DDT's effects on fish tissues, found the dangers of PCB lurking there as well. Soon its presence was discovered in New Bedford harbor sediments and many other parts of the environment.

Monsanto was the only company in the U.S. to make PCBs. Four years went by before Monsanto informed its wholesale customers that PCBs had some environmental dangers, that they should curtail sales to open systems which used the chemical. In 1976 the Toxic Substances Control Act legislated PCB out of existence. Monsanto ceased manufacture almost immediately. Neither the government nor the company moved to recall the huge amount of PCB now in circulation. Instead, the EPA authorized its continued use. O'Neill concedes the product's damaging effects on health but does not agree that it is a proven carcinogen.

In 1977–78, the two plants on the Acushnet stopped using PCB. Mysteriously, PCB levels in the harbor did not drop. The chemical apparently had attached itself to sediments in the sewers and stayed there. Fresh sewage passing through takes some PCB along. In this way, 200 to 700 pounds a year swish their way into Buzzards Bay. "What we have here is an uncontrolled PCB problem in an aquatic system," says EPA's man in charge of PCBs in New Bedford.

The government seems all but paralyzed by the terrors of New Bedford's harbor. Studies pile upon studies. The gross contamination of New Bedford's river, harbor, and estuary is well documented. PCB levels in fish and shellfish therein are shown to be dangerous for people to eat, but there is no action.

Attention turns to people who are eating the fish and shellfish which eat PCB-flavored plankton. A 1981 study of the blood of

New Bedford's frequent fisheaters shows them to be "among the highest PCB-contaminated people in the U.S.," the Weaver report says. A second blood test a year later, in cooperation with the Center for Disease Control in Atlanta, Georgia, has approximately the same result. A third set of blood tests designed by the Atlanta Center, is examining what happens over several years to people with high levels of PCB pulsing through their arteries. One hopes that results will conform with Costakes' sentiment that no one ever dies from PCBs.

U.S. officialdom has not exactly raced to prevent the PCB danger ahead. In the early '70s it set the safe limit of PCB in tissues at 5 ppm, then found that the much-studied chemical was even more toxic than had been estimated. It was now known to affect liver function, reproduction, and to cause tumors. Upping tolerance to 2 ppm was proposed. It would, the FDA said, significantly reduce risk to consumers without harming fisheries. The FDA received 100 comments on this proposal from fisheries and consumer groups. Later the National Fisheries Institute—the ubiquitous trade organization—objected and asked for a hearing.

After years, the "safe" level had its formal hearing before an FDA administrative judge. The antagonists were the FDA's Bureau of Foods versus the National Fisheries Institute (industry), supported by the National Marine Fisheries Service (government). The argument concerned not health but cash money. The FDA had said that changing the tolerance level from 5 ppm to 2 ppm would incur only a $10 million to $15 million loss a year. The opposition said that loss would more likely be $200 million, an unacceptable economic blow, they claimed, to hardworking fishermen and profit-making fisheries.

The FDA judge in his wisdom selected a figure of $86 million and sent the whole record along to the top man in FDA, its commissioner, for a decision in 1982. There has been no decision and there is no date by which one is required. Meanwhile, on the

150

basis of the latest studies, it is widely agreed that 2 ppm is all the PCB we can take.

Eight years after the Woods Hole scientist spotted the soaring PCB levels in New Bedford waters, the town was nominated for Superfund status, one of 17,000 locations in the U.S.A. asking for federal help from the EPA's Superfund for hazardous conditions.

The fund has $1.6 billion, mostly from taxes on the manufacture of certain chemicals and petroleum. The government uses the money to respond to the presence of hazardous substances that may "endanger the public health and welfare," the EPA says. The "responsible party" has to help; the state pays 10 percent of the cost, Superfund pays for the rest of cleaning up the dangerous condition.

New Bedford has the dubious honor of being one of 546 places to qualify for Superfund cleanup. Since there is enough money to clean up only 200 sites in the nation, each state must choose its top priority. New Bedford won that contest, too.

The EPA spent the year making Superfund studies in New Bedford. In July, 1983, it completed a Remedial Action Master Plan, "outlining investigations needed to determine the full extent of cleanup required." Next a feasibility study. It will take between fifteen and thirty months, the EPA says, to design a strategy, if, indeed, any is possible, another year or more to try the clean up. The cost, about $7 million.

One of many hot spots in the grossly contaminated Acushnet is about a mile long and the width of the river. Here PCB level is a momentous 190,000 ppm. What to do? Dredge, and you have to find a place for contaminated spoils. Cover the hot spot over, and in twenty years the PCBs will seep out again. Incinerate, bury, move it somewhere else—all seem impossible for such an enormous volume. "The search is for the 'most feasible' remedy," EPA's spokesman says, "the action that is cost effective and protects the environment and human health and welfare." That is a large order. The troubling words are "cost effective." How much is too much to make the old fishing port safe for fish and its fish safe for people once again?

While we consider this and other questions, there is still no action.

In the meantime, PCB is most likely moving out into the ocean. Any assumption that it will stay quietly in the harbor defies all natural laws. Out beyond the bay, PCB will be spread far and wide by the fish that eat it. New Bedford is the worst yet documented, but not the only, place where such contamination is building up, where PCBs flow slowly out to sea.

Two General Electric plants dumped PCB into the upper stretches of New York's Hudson River for years, until officially stopped. Many of the fish spawned there emerged into New Jersey waters where, in 1982, the state concluded that PCB was more concentrated in saltwater than freshwater fish, particularly striped bass, bluefish, Atlantic sturgeon, white perch, and American eels. New Jersey issued an advisory warning to residents to limit amounts of these fish that they eat, to trim away skin, dark meat, fat, where PCB is stored, to broil, rather than fry, allowing fat to run off fish tissues. New York issued a similar health advisory. In 1983, Rhode Island became alarmed. Then the *Boston Globe*, after a quick bluefish survey, found enough PCB contamination to persuade the commonwealth's Department of Public Health to make a two-month study.

Another study. This one discovered highest PCB levels in larger fish in the Nantucket and Vineyard Sounds—average 2.9 ppm— and in Buzzards Bay—average 2.3 ppm—somewhat lower around Cape Ann, Boston Harbor, and Cape Cod Bay. Pressured by the publicity, Massachusetts' Public Health Department issued its advisory warning to citizens.

The decade of inaction sounds a loud alarm. It tells us that in the present state of the art of ocean management, we are unable to restore the ecosystem to its balance within a minimum of a dozen years. Even with the unusual advantages New Bedford has had of topflight science from Woods Hole and elsewhere, detailed information piled up in a stack of studies, and Superfund funds, the happy balance of the aquarium seems beyond our reach.

Managing the sea escapes us. Keeping fish healthy, central to the whole, is a measure of what we understand about the monumental task. We see New Bedford's effort to control the demise of haddock started with a straightforward biological goal, diluted by conflicting interests until it was compromised beyond recognition. We see sea scallops decline, striped bass diminish. We stand by helplessly as within the span of one generation PCBs are invented, distributed, dumped into the waters, and are accumulated in marine life.

As this book goes to press, a conference of biologists and conservationists announces that "emergency measures" are needed to save striped bass from extinction. Participants discussed legislation with aides to the Senate Majority Leader Howard H. Baker, Jr., came away with the impression that "a moratorium was not likely in the immediate future." But the U.S. Attorney's office has sued six corporations for polluting the waters off New Bedford by releasing PCBs into the New Bedford Harbor. Among those named are Aerovax, Inc., and Cornell-Dubilier Electronics Co. The suit was filed under the Superfund bill.

We suffer the suicidal tendency to try to hide the changes we have made in fish habitats. The New Bedford Chamber of Commerce encourages visitors to go clamming although shellfish beds lie suffused with toxic PCB, urges fishing although docks are built out into deadly waters. Monsanto, producer of PCB, takes its time, when there is no time to waste, to advise its customers of PCB dangers. The regional council in charge hires no scientists and does not listen to those who volunteer.

We suffer the tendency to gamble if there is money to be made. Harvest lobsters in the toxic waters, an official advises. Perhaps people won't eat them too regularly to get sick. Keep the PCB tolerance level at 5 ppm, the federal guardian of our food and drugs orders. The money lost in telling the truth that it is 2 ppm or maybe even 1 ppm is too high a price to pay. Keep using existing PCBs; they are still profitable. The U.S. bureaucracy gambles citizens' survival against citizens' cash money from the sea. Money wins.

We need to see the risks laid out straight, recognizable, inescapable. New Bedford, in microcosm, directs the eye to a vital section of the ocean that has come under our aegis. The peril is as real, close to home, as it is in the town on Buzzards Bay. In the face of such terror, our only choice is to try to make the ocean safe.

10
THE POSSIBILITY

On a bitter winter day when the wind blusters and ice covers the ground, on a walk in the snow where a drift suddenly traps your body in a frigid embrace, on a ski run which takes you out of sight of civilization over a treeless ice-covered mountain, these are times when you can imagine majestic Antarctica, home of the South Pole, lying off by itself at the bottom of the world. The continent is covered with ice a mile thick, surrounded by ice shelves and, in the winter, by enough pack ice to double its size. Flat-top icebergs break off from time to time, move at the mercy of the wild roaring Southern Ocean, where winds blow with cyclone force to pile up the roughest waters anywhere in the world.

This turbulent icy sea is the kingdom of warm-blooded marine mammals which once ruled it in extraordinary profusion. An explorer, sailing cautiously into an ice-walled bay, came upon a primordial sight, a herd of blue whales, the largest animals in the world, each as big as thirty average-size elephants. They appeared to be playing, blowing, diving, arching their great graceful forms. The freezing roiling water is home to several baleen whale species besides the blues, to emperor penguins and smaller Adelie penguins, fish, squid, seabirds. The land, not surprisingly, is almost lifeless except for a few lichens hidden in rocks under the ice, although cumbersome elephant seals and fur seals come ashore to breed.

Antarctica—continent and ocean—is, from one perspective, the most valuable region in the world. It is not a place where you

157

would want to settle down or to buy real estate should it be for sale. Antarctica has a weightier worth. It could become the one almost pure place left on the globe. Most contemporary pressures push against its existence in this pristine state. Most are blind to the enormity of its value.

Antarctica is necessary as a sentinel of what was and what might be again. Its pollution is still minimal enough that global change can be measured. It supplies the world with clean cold bottom water. And it is the habitat for a matchless multitude of wildlife.

This is the moment in which men will decide Antarctica's future. If rationality triumphs, we will have made a start toward a viable ocean for tomorrow.

"A region of almost unparalleled interest," participants in the International Geophysical Year in 1957 described Antarctica. Forty scientific stations were established during the Year, studies of many Antarctic aspects begun. The U.S., for one, had twelve ships, 3,000 men, and sent home 27 tons of data. In 1961, the Antarctic Treaty was put into force by twelve nations which agreed that Antarctica "shall continue forever to be used exclusively for peaceful purposes." There is a Scientific Committee on Antarctic Research, another on Oceanic Research, and recently an agreement on Conservation of Antarctic Marine Living Resources. Barbara Mitchell, an authority on affairs Antarctic, says these are drafted with "the technique of deliberate ambiguity." While ambiguous phrasing has kept Antarctic peace for more than twenty years, it cannot settle the hard conflicts now approaching.

The power to run the place belongs to the Club, as nonmembers are likely to refer to the group of original treaty signers plus four added members. Eight have staked out slices of the frozen pie for themselves, eight, including the U.S. and the USSR, recognize no claims. The two latest additions—India and Brazil—have both done research in Antarctica, both match Club members' sophistication in environmental protection. Brazil has a zone-of-interest claim. India is of particular significance because, as leader of the Third World, its admission indicates a new willingness on the part of the Club to recognize qualified Third World nations. Under the Club's aegis, scientific research proceeds apace; 2,000 scientists recently wintered over, studying such diverse subjects as the extent of DDT in penguin shells, Antarctica's effect on world climate, and, unannounced, the possibilities of harvestable oil. Bacterial decomposition is very prolonged in the extreme cold. Litter lasts for years. "There is," a returning scientist says, "a slow filthifying under way."

Antarctica has been dramatically altered by the massive slaughter of whales and seals. Given a chance, its ecosystem might recover. It could then give us a standard—the ecosystem standard—for decisions about this region. The reasoning behind such decisions could eventually be applied to the entire ocean.

Only the ecosystem standard makes sense. Dealing with one element of the sea or another has consistently failed to work. A natural ecosystem does work. There is a lot to learn about Antarctica, about its essential parts and how they interlock. Whales, for example, brought to the edge of extinction here, might be able to restore themselves if we do not interfere with their essential Antarctic habitat.

The results of whales' revival could be awesome. These large-brained animals have an intelligence we know very little about. They function on a different plane from ours, with different drives, different mechanisms for achievement. From whales we might learn a happier, more peaceable way of life. The pain of our long love-hate relation with the monarch of the sea might at last be resolved in the cleansing freeze of Antarctica.

Wild speculation? Perhaps. But not beyond the limits of credulity, even attainment.

A start has been made at the ecosystem approach in regions of the ocean which were in such bad shape that surrounding nations resolved to do something about them. Secluded seas like the Mediterranean and Baltic which have become grossly polluted,

159

inspire efforts to clean up the whole mess, recapture the natural balance, reclaim the waters. As will be seen, the enormity of the task makes progress slow. Still, plans are being made for ten troubled seas—the Caribbean, Persian Gulf, Red Sea, and others—and still, people hope that plans will come true.

With restoration of its populace, Antarctica could be a prime functioning ecosystem once again. It does not need to be reclaimed or restored like the ten seas, New Bedford, or the New York Bight. But our intrusion must stop before it gets going too fast.

Two resources are the apples in this frosted Eden. One is the possibility of taking oil from the continental shelf, some 400 to 800 meters deep compared to the world average of 133 meters. Digging, processing, transporting oil in Antarctica will have all the usual dangers for the ecosystem except that here, the danger is much multiplied by the conditions and the temperature.

More immediate and agonizingly *au point* is the human desire for the key food of the Antarctic. Whales, seals, penguins, birds, fish, and squid all depend on a protein-rich, 2-inch red shrimplike creature, *Euphasia superba*, or krill (Norwegian for "tiny fish"). By nature's design, there is a huge supply of krill in the Southern Ocean. A blue whale, for example, can eat its required 4 tons of krill a day and find plenty awaiting it on the morrow.

Now man wants krill for himself.

To get it he will have to fish offshore of the "coldest, windiest, highest, dryest continent in the world," as it is described in Barbara Mitchell's excellent briefing document. Everything in Antarctica is big scale; the land itself is bigger than the U.S. and Mexico combined. Its vast ice plateau is 13,000 feet high. A series of mountains push up through the ice and snow in West Antarctica, thought vulnerable to the coming greenhouse effect. Should Antarctic ice melt in the west, only a series of isolated islands would remain. The eastern half of the continent would be mountainous land with a deep central lake. If all Antarctic ice melts, the ocean will rise an estimated 150 to 300 feet. The rise would flood coast cities, ripple over roofs from New York's City Hall to San Francisco's venerable Fairmont Hotel, put most American homes under water.

It is dark in Antarctica in its winter, March through September. But when spring arrives, the sun comes out, highlighting the sparkling crystal mountains and brilliant white plains. Above this frozen fantasia, the sky is bright and endlessly blue, without a trace of pollution in the air, a fact much remarked on by recent visitors.

The spring sun brings about a primeval benevolence in the Southern Ocean, a vernal outburst of krill in huge shoals which can be 5 kilometers long, great red patches in the sea. Average standing stocks, according to Professor Sayed Z. El-Sayed, a krill expert, and others, are between 200 million metric tons and 650 million metric tons a year, a lot of tiny fish. The National Science Foundation reports that in 1981, scientists on the R/V *Melville* measured one school of krill several square miles around and from 60 to 600 feet deep. This single largest mass ever measured was 10 million metric tons of krill, as much as about one-seventh of the entire annual world catch of fish and shellfish. At night the krill lights up, an observer says, "a mass of living blue-green fire in the water."

Krill's production line is admirable natural engineering. On the ocean surface the current moves north until it meets warmer water pushed southward by prevailing winds. The two collide in the aptly named Antarctic Convergence. Here nutrients and heat from the northern waters mix with the frigid Antarctic current. The latter, now warmer than before, makes a reverse dive to travel back to its place of origin via a bottom current. When it hits the ice wall rearing up from the deep, it surfaces, sheds its warmth and nutrients in the cold sunny waters (a mechanism not unlike the upwelling which fed the anchovetas in Peru) and starts its journey north once more, a liquid freight train on a parabolic circular track.

In the warm months when the train delivers its goods, a

161

certain microscopic plankton thrives on the nutrients and bursts into abundant bloom. This is food for *Euphasia superba*, enabling its colossal production which feeds the entire Antarctic populace. The process is specially intriguing because it is the shortest possible food chain producing animal protein; nutrient to plant to krill, ready for eating. Not too long ago, investigators discovered that krill may not be as devotedly vegetarian as had been thought. It has, El-Sayed says, carniverous and cannibalistic habits that transform even more energy into food for the Antarctic population.

Blue whales and other baleen species—bowheads, fin whales, gray whales—are built for krill eating, in contrast to the toothed whales, which bite and chew their food. Grazing on the krill fields, the whale opens its huge mouth, within which, on each side, are baleen plates that look like slats, equipped with bristles to keep the krill in, while the whale, with its 3-ton tongue, forces water out through its closed lips. The leviathans are hungry after the winter's meager forage up north and eat ceaselessly, storing the food in their bodies against the coming winter migration to warmer waters where they breed. Blue whales are not the only krill consumers in Antarctica. Crabeater seals, despite their name, fur seals, minke whales, seven species of penguins, and seabirds all live mostly on krill.

The whales once consumed some 190 million tons of krill a year. Now the figure is estimated at 50 or 60 million tons because of the twentiety-century whale slaughter. Some nations figure that the result is a 140-million-ton surplus, and they might as well catch it, an example of one-species thinking is a severe ecosystem risk. Nevertheless, the Soviets and Japanese pioneered a krill harvest. Today there is krill meal for pigs and cattle; for people, krill butter, krill cheese spread, a Japanese fish sausage which is 20 percent krill, and Okean, which you can buy in Moscow supermarkets "to enrich paté and deviled eggs."

Competition for krill grows. So do the dangers of harvesting it. Reducing krill swarms might inhibit krill breeding completely, a scientist says. Reducing krill numbers could deplete populations which depend on it—seals, penguins—slow the recovery of slaughtered species, the blue, fin, humpback, and sei whales. So far, krill in the Southern Ocean is still abundant, not known to be close to the situation of anchovetas in Peru, but an increased harvest could move toward it. Man's memory is short.

The decision to harvest krill was made by the USSR and by Japan in the 1970s, partly because, like the mountain to climb, the krill were there to be caught, partly to give their distant fishing boats, expelled from the EEZ off other nations' coasts, a way to amortize capital investments, and partly to test whether a profitable market for krill could be developed.

The decision to look for oil in the Antarctic was made around the same time. There is an estimate by the U.S. Geological Survey of 45,000 million barrels in the continental shelf, another by Gulf Oil in 1979 for 50,000 million barrels, James Barnes says in *Let's Save Antarctica*. The first serious seismic exploration, a three-year project, began in 1981 by the Japan Natural Oil Corporation. The sixteen nations in the Club eye this Pandora's box with more than casual interest. They are not alone.

Most experts believe that oil is there. The frozen continent was once part of the supercontinent Pangaea and eventually separated from it by continental drift. It is likely to have the same structure, including oil- and gas-bearing rock, as its former neighbor, Australia, also separated from that first landmass. To find out whether there is enough oil to warrant development is the first step in a potentially explosive multination negotiation.

The U.S. proposes an international regime covering the possibility of finding and getting Antarctic oil. William Brown, specialist in Antarctic affairs at the Environmental Defense Fund, comments that the U.S. and other nations considered making Antarctica a sanctuary, but have ruled out that option. One reason given is the world need for oil. Other reasons, Brown says, are "political factors, especially those concerning territorial claims." The 1982 Environmental Impact Statement on the proposal says mineral exploitation will be an asset as long as there are no unacceptable environmental risks. It does not define "unacceptable."

The Club considers the U.S. proposal along with others. Its meetings are private but Brown and fellow knowledgeable observers agree that the Consultative Parties are trying to come to an agreement "as a matter of urgency."

Both decisions—taking krill and taking oil—are momentous when set in a more expansive time frame, the grandeur of an ancient heritage.

Two hundred years ago, no one had ever seen Antarctica. We must take it on faith plus a good deal of solid geological evidence, that the massive ice cap, the wild frigid waters, the awesome concordance of marine mammals, and their spectacular food supply existed through the millennia, thriving, primeval. Captain James Cook of the British Royal Navy made three trips to the Antarctic Circle in the 1770s, each time to be pushed back by heavy masses of pack ice without a glimpse of the continent. A Russian and an American are the first to have sighted the land in 1820, after which it was mapped and explored in hopes of finding the South Pole.

Exploring was so difficult that the nineteenth century was called Antarctica's Heroic Age. One commentator believes the explorers exaggerated descriptions of their anguish and suffering "to give them the look of heroes," thus moving their patrons to raise their salaries. One who does not fit that cynical note is Robert Scott, who, searching for the South Pole, froze to death with three companions on the return journey, just 11 miles from a depot. The Norwegian Roald Amundsen had beaten Scott to the Pole and, in surprising cruelty for a winner, left him a note in the dark silk tent he erected over the spot.

Long before the explorers, the populace of the Southern Ocean, unique among all animal life, had moved in. They are unique because some eons back, these mammals, for reasons of their own, turned away from their terrestrial habitats to live in the ocean. It is a dramatic and still mysterious evolution. Three billion or more years ago life began in some warm secluded spot in the sea, eons later crawled up on land where it began to diversify and many eons after that, some air-breathing, milk-giving, warm-blooded mammals turned around and went back to live in the water again. Of all these, the cetaceans—whales and dolphins—made the most complete turnabout, living their entire life in the sea. Others, like seals and sea lions, come onto land to breed and deliver their young. Not whales. They have no external structure to support them; a beached whale crushes itself to death with its own weight.

A whale is as streamlined as its piscatorial companions in the ocean, so much so that for a long time, man thought the leviathan which swallowed Jonah to be a very large fish. This was before its still sketchy but well-grounded evolution had been worked out.

"The period in which ancestors of whales turned toward the water was an evolutionary hothouse," Robert McNally says in *So Remorseless a Havoc*. "Dinosaurs were extinct, mammals evolved fast to fill the dinosaur gap, forerunners of horses, elephants, other primates appeared." There are no fossils of primitive whales, but piecing the development together, they seem to have evolved from large piglike creatures. Seals probably had bearlike ancestors; sea otter ancestors are crab-eating land otters.

In different parts of the world and at different times in history, the ancient life forms we will never see probably took up residence near lakes and rivers and foraged in the water for food, McNally says. The primitive hooved animals that would become cetaceans began to acquire the necessary equipment for aquatic existence. "Their respiratory, circulatory, locomotory, thermoregulatory and communicative systems are all significantly different from the typical terrestrial mammalian pattern," an expert says. Arranging to breathe, move, keep warm and communicate in the three-dimensional ocean mass took time. Seals acquired heavy fur coats to keep them warm; whales evolved an underskin layer of fat and muscle sinews known as blubber. When they were ready, in another ten million years or so, they splashed in to stay.

165

Only their mammality did not change. Fascinating evidence of mammal descent is currently found in whale embryos. "Unborn whales early in their development look much the same as other mammalian embryos, humans included," McNally says. "Rudimentary legs appear, nostrils open at the tip of the snout, genitals develop on the body surface. Then the changes begin. . . ."

Forelimbs change to flippers; the remains of five fingers are enclosed in fibrous tissue. Breathing is through a blowhole on the top of the head; eyes are small. Seeing is not nearly as important to a whale as hearing; they navigate by the echoes of their sounds— clicks and squeaks—and communicate in a fashion still not decoded by the nonstop communicator *Homo sapiens*.

Cetaceans and elephants are the only mammals with mental equipment and big brains corresponding to those of humans. Our superiority in being able to exterminate the other two species is on the record, but Sterling Bunnell, psychiatrist, says, "intelligence has many possible dimensions, and in some of these we may be less advanced than certain big-brained non-manipulators." Dr. Bunnell says efforts to understand the minds of cetaceans have been "sporadic and feeble," and that we know very little about how they use their heads. "Could it be that some of the undiscovered possibilities which would be most valuable to us have long been known to our fellow mammals of the sea?

"I believe we should stop killing whales except for human survival," Dr. Victor Scheffer, former chairman, U.S. Marine Mammal Commission, says. "[Whales] live in families, play in the moonlight, talk to one another, and care for one another in distress. They are awesome and mysterious. In their cold, wet and forbidding world they are complete and successful. They deserve to be saved, not as potential meatballs, but as a source of encouragement for mankind."

Interest intensifies. Maybe the whales have a thought system we could use. But butchery comes first in our development.

As early as the ninth century, whales were harpooned off

Norway. In the twelfth century the Basques, borrowing Norwegian toolmaking, killed "right" whales migrating along their shores. First they killed for villagers' subsistence. Discovering that whale oil and baleen were marketable items, they went into the whaling business, hunted right whales till there were no more in the area, then bowheads, which soon disappeared as well. This wipe-out-the-species pattern was followed by many other European nations. Across the sea, the Japanese, too, killed one Pacific whale species after another, quitting each when it had declined too far to be profitable hunting. Yankee whaling started in the seventeenth century with whales close to shore—rights and grays—expanded in the eighteenth century with larger boats, hunting in the ocean for the sperm whale with its white waxy spermaceti, which made bright-burning candles, its ambergris for perfume, ivory from its teeth.

By mid-nineteenth century the Yankee whalers were killing 8,000 to 10,000 whales a year, earning more than $10 million harvesting whale oil and baleen. By the time they stopped, they had killed about half a million great whales in all; of these, one species became extinct, another is close to it, and the rest were so greatly reduced that they were not worth going whaling for.

The big, powerful baleen whales—the blues, finbacks, sei whales—were too fast for sailing ships and hand-thrown harpoons. Killing whales was soon advanced by technology with which to conquer the giants. Steam power was harnessed in the mid-nineteenth century. Then, Sven Foyn, Norwegian sealer, contrived a cannon that fired a heavy harpoon, tipped with a grenade, McNally says. "As the harpoon crashed into the whale, a glass vial of sulfuric acid broke and detonated the grenade inside the animal's body, shredding its innards with shock and shrapnel."

With this weapon mounted on steamships, there were new whale worlds to conquer. A Norwegian whaling expedition was the first to attack the greatest gathering of wildlife on this globe, greater, even, than on the plains of Africa or America, an estimated 800,000 huge whales in Antarctic waters. Despite experience elsewhere, there

167

was no rule of caution to prevent overwhaling, just a pell-mell rush to kill, process, sell the products.

In the year 1910–11, 10,500 Antarctic humpbacks were killed in the Southern Ocean; in 1926, less than 100 could be found. In 1930–31, 125,000 huge blues were killed; ten years later the take was less than half. The blues calved every two years on average. There was no way that they could keep up their population level with the soaring rate of killing. Nor was there any place they could go to escape, tied as they were to the uniquely gigantic food supply. After World War II, the figures of precipitous decline of whales were published by a renowned cetologist. The alarming facts had the amazing effect of *stepping up* the Antarctic whale take, each whaler trying to kill as many of the remaining whales as possible.

Since 1940, 2,234,000 whales have been slaughtered, more than all the whales man has ever killed throughout history.

Today big-scale whaling is uneconomic.

It is hard to believe that it has happened so quickly. Species after species, whales have been decimated, ever more efficiently. It took 500 years to reach the nonprofit point for right whales, a century or so for sperm whales, fifty years for all but a few bowheads in the Arctic, thirty years for humpbacks. Blue whales, greatest animal on the globe, were brought close to extinction in just fifteen years. In 1948–49, 7,781 were killed; in 1958, 1,500; in 1964, twenty.

Fourteen governments set up the International Whaling Commission (IWC) in 1946 "to safeguard for future generations the great natural resources represented by whale stocks." IWC failure to do what it set as its goal is a sorry tale of international politics and barefaced greed. Suffice it to say that almost thirty years went by while whales continued to be killed in profusion. Finally the U.S. proposed a moratorium on the butchery. It took ten years, threats of embargo on fish from Norway and Japan, thousands of more whales killed until finally, in 1982, it was agreed that whaling will cease in 1986. Japan, the Soviet Union, Norway and several smaller countries objected, and said they would continue to permit whaling. The U.S. is applying heavy pressure on Japan to stop whaling by reducing its allocation of U.S. fish. Private groups also boycott Norwegian fish products. "The whaling industry," Greenpeace says, "will go down fighting—we can't ever forget that— but it will go down."

What are we killing whales for? Every saleable part of a whale now has a better, cheaper substitute. Had we understood the threat to Antarctica's entire schemata in losing whales, we might have been willing to shift capital investment out of the water slaughter and whales would be there for us, today. Perhaps they still can be. Their revival is in part up to us.

Choice is based on emotion as well as intellect. A sense of tenderness for whales emerges. Some call it the other side of guilt for what we have done to our fellow brainy mammals, others believe it the revival of a prehistoric bond, some shadowy recognition of need for each other, now that we stand to lose the species from the globe. This interspecies love takes many forms. In *Moby Dick*, the classic whale tale, Melville's story line is suffused with awe of whales joined with compassion. In admiration, he describes a whale's regular rising to the surface to breathe, which "exposes him to all the fatal hazards of the chase. For not by hook or by net could this vast leviathan be caught, when sailing a thousand fathoms beneath the sunlight. Not so much thy skill then, O hunter, as the great necessities that strike victory to thee!"

Love of some sort may be the spark that urges us to rescue whales from extinction. There is no guarantee that rescue can succeed among species that have been as drastically reduced as the blues have, for example, but there is every reason to try. The huge krill-eating whales are of particular importance to the Antarctic ecosystem. Whales keep its equilibrium intact. Without their abundance, the animal balance changes. Fur seals increase dramatically, tempting man to new slaughter, as do penguins and seabirds. The small minke whale, the one survivor of the whale holocaust, being thought too small to bother slaughtering, now multiplies with renewed vigor, having more krill to eat. No one knows what the effect on the ecosystem will be when new species begin to fill the whale void.

Removing the great whales was the first major intrusion into the Antarctic ecosystem. Next was removing krill. There is no real krill quota, just a general agreement that man will take what has been left by the whales. One trouble is that nobody knows how much that may be. "There is no accurate data base as yet," El-Sayed says. Another trouble: suppose whales come back without consultation with the human harvesters of their food? Suppose there must be a quick change of policy, giving up krill for the whales' sake? The record carries no hint that industrialized nations would act as one, fast, to withdraw from krill competition, particularly with whales, who do not fight back.

For a healthy ecosystem, krill must flourish as it will, supporting the animal populace of the waters. Krill is their sole source of nourishment. Under these circumstances, our desire for it abjures rationality.

Exploring for, digging for, and removing oil from Antarctica is the third attack on the ecosystem which, for so many millennia, functioned in its pure icy state. Unlike whales and krill, oil will soon be gone from the globe. It is not a matter of choice. Even a generous oil field discovered in Antarctica will not keep the world oil-powered very much longer.

There are no oil wells in Antarctica at this writing. But there are signs that they are on the way. The Club is close to a plan for regulating mineral development. There is a proposal, supported by Friends of the Earth International and the World Wildlife Fund, to make Antarctica the first World Park, an idea which the Club rejected out of hand. The powerful Club nations firmly declare that this is not a common area, that the Common Heritage of Mankind concept which made so much trouble for the dreamed-of

170

mining of manganese nodules, does not apply to this region. "There is no existing binding agreement to limit oil activities," Bill Brown says. The Sierra Club reports that the Treaty nations are "moving quickly to conclude a legal agreement on possible mineral development in Antarctica. . . ." to head off Third World interest. The Club is now considering a draft of an oil agreement.

Oil from the frozen seas will cost us the ecosystem. To clean up oil in the Antarctic is much harder than in warmer areas, Barbara Mitchell says in *Frozen Stakes*, her recent Antarctic survey. Oil might not break down, or it might emulsify, become incorporated into the ice and be widely dispersed. Microbial degradation of oil takes much longer in the cold. A spill would have severe effects on marine life, particularly krill. Oil, penetrating the sea, would show up far from Antarctica, carried by deep circulation to the bottom waters of the world. "The arguments for proceeding with caution are strong," Mitchell says.

Elsewhere, one-time wilderness seas have been beset upon by civilization to the point of killing conditions for marine life and for people. Nations surrounding the Mediterranean, Baltic, and other seas are desperate to restore the dread polluted waters to a pure working ecosystem once again. Reconstruction is a job of unimagined difficulty. Even partial success may be beyond our present abilities.

In the Mediterranean, 90 percent of the sewage from 44 million people who live around the sea plus 100 million tourists who crowd its beaches in the summer is sent untreated into Homer's fabled wine-dark waters. Poisonous industrial pollutants from land-based industry, toxic chemical compounds and oil from the ceaseless parade of tankers add to the degradation. At fifty shellfish stations offshore four countries, only 3 percent to 4 percent are safe for human consumption. Swimmers, enjoying the Mediterranean warmth, stay immersed longer than usual, giving themselves more exposure to disease. Cholera outbreaks are now frequent. Many waterborne diseases with long incubation periods are rife: viral hepatitis, typhoid, poliomyelitis, dysentery. Symptoms show up weeks after the swimmer, mystified and ill, is back at home.

The 1970s was a decade of alarm, studies, adoption of an action plan. By 1980, almost all Mediterranean countries agreed to stop pollution and help clean up the sea. They say they will control release of mercury, lead, used motor oil; sewage, detergents, carcinogens; radioactive wastes. Implementing this agreement will cost member states $10 billion to $15 billion over the next decade or longer. Whether the Mediterranean's enclosed ecosystem can recover will not be known until at least the 1990s. In many inlets and coves the damage already appears irreversible.

The Baltic is a shallow cold brackish sea, stratified, with the saltier water below, relatively fresh water above. The long turnover time of the water makes the Baltic sensitive to an increased load of nutrients, and the bottom is likely to get stagnant, losing its oxygen. This precarious balance attracted attention in the 1960s, enough attention to achieve a political concensus to clean up the sea. In 1974, the Helsinki Convention made sweeping resolves to restore the entire ecosystem.

Sweden started cleaning up sewage dumped into the Baltic, other nations followed. Some ports built facilities to encourage ship captains to obey no-dump regulations. A Fisheries Commission, formed in 1975, divides the Baltic's shores into zones with the Norse version of management councils in charge. Some beaches, closed for years, now welcome politicians for a swim in front of TV cameras. Many more years are needed to clean up the remains of decades of pollution on the sea floor and achieve healthy fish again. The Baltic ecosystem wavers toward somewhat better health. "If our plan is successful," an official says, "the Baltic environmental policies may serve as a model for the rest of the world." Will there be time?

Pollution in the Mediterranean, a documentary made in France in 1980, films the dying sea. "Skin divers are shown swimming through clouds of suspended particles of excrement and household waste which settle on the sea floor in an indescribable unforgetta- ble mush," one reviewer says. "Dead fish lie on the sands. Only a few species survive, most strikingly black leathery-looking starfish . . . a nightmarish glimpse of the future." Viewers watch scum from Marseille's sewage spreading along the coast, further each day, meeting up with scum from other coast centers. It is hard to be- lieve that with the best will in the world man can restore this eco- system before it dies.

There are many such seas, many well-meaning plans, many small successes. But the big inexorable motion is toward ailing ecosystems, failing ecosystems, disregarded through the years, dying while we try, at least in some places, to undo the violence we have visited on these ocean regions.

Antarctica does not have to go the degradation route. Now that we know without doubt where this route leads, an insight that was never as blazingly clear before, Antarctica becomes The Pos- sibility, the one chance, with the whales' cooperation, to keep a pure place in the ocean. It can be a beacon, showing us what the ocean can be again, lest we forget while watching underwater films of the Mediterranean. To give up this clean, strong ecosystem for a mess of krill or a momentary fortune in oil is myopic madness.

The Club's tight grip on Antarctica is being challenged. Third World countries, which insisted on the right to share in Law of the Sea plans for mining the deep, now assert a right to a place on Antarctic councils. At the U.N. they made a forceful appeal. Ant- arctica controls the world's weather, they said, so should be in the care of the entire world, and its resources should be shared by the world. In December, 1983, the U.N. agreed to make a compre- hensive study of Antarctica.

This has set off a political and philosophical debate on the ethics of Third World participation which requires, and has in- spired, books of its own. Pros and cons for Antarctica apply here. The positive aspects of this new U.N. involvement is that it might

173

put pressure on the Club to be more open in its dealings, keeping the world informed of its stewardship. On the other side, many say that the Club will do a better job of governance than all U.N. members together. Being more sophisticated in environmental matters, there is a better chance that it will see the difficulties of exploitation.

The Club or the U.N. or both might understand the extraordinary value of returning Antarctica to its pristine state. The heroic age of the frozen land and sea has yet to come. Uncompromising protection could bring it about. If it does, everybody would be a hero.

11
PUT THE OCEAN FIRST

How long do we want a viable ocean? Fifty years, a hundred, five hundred? An impossible question to a society which takes a well-functioning ocean for granted. No generation before us has had to consider this question. But we have brought the ocean to the point that taking it for granted is no longer even a possibility. You know that as you hesitate, now, to dig a clam, eat a fish, take a swim in the sea, not sure that it is safe.

With perception and resolute care we might be able to salvage a somewhat damaged but still working ocean for this planet to carry with it on its journey in space. It would be a magnificent achievement to preserve the sea. If we do, there might be unending generations of life in the ocean and the everlasting potential of life on earth which the ocean makes possible. Saving the ocean from ourselves will not be easy but at great cost it can be done. The cost is partly in resources of the sea that have been ours for the taking. Even more, the cost is in labor of the mind, the gigantic effort required to reverse the way we regard the ocean.

Perhaps the end will come first by a nuclear holocaust launched from one of the huge new submarines sailing "a thousand fathoms beneath the sunlight" as did Melville's whale. But should we manage to put aside nuclear weapons, we will meet the same fate, if somewhat postponed, from the sea. A killing sea will be Neptune's revenge for our misuse of his domain—unless we can act with determination, fast.

The idea that man's comfort and convenience come first in using the ocean brings us too close to disaster to tolerate. Man's very existence is at stake. For this we must surrender present priorities and put the requirements of the ocean first. In gentler times, man used the ocean as he wished with no ill effects. But in these years of technological triumph, population explosion, and inexhaustible determination to grow, our society's desires are rapacious enough to destroy the sea, and eventually life on earth.

The ocean can no longer be responsive to our every wish for its resources. It cannot be a dump for toxics, raw sewage, radioactive submarines. There is no such thing as its "unreasonable degradation," a concept which some ocean laws enunciate. The sea is either degraded or it is not degraded. No degree of degradation is reasonable if the ocean is to survive. It has no "assimilative capacity" for what we put into it, another soothing pleasantry we allow ourselves. Man and fish may survive 2 parts per million of a toxic in the sea. One part per million would be safer. You never know when 1 will increase to, 2, 5, or 10. For a viable ocean, choose zero.

Putting the ocean first is a rigorous discipline. Short-term, it seems unnecessary to deprive ourselves of one small sewage outfall pipe in the bay, of an occasional pulse-fishing expedition, or harvesting a share of superabundant krill in Antarctica. But when the ocean comes first, decisions must be made taking slow ocean time into account.

Action-reaction becomes action—long pause—reaction. On ocean time, it might be years, decades, before effects of what is put into the ocean or taken out of it can be measured. The sea requires us to think far ahead, to make long-term decisions. What we do today will matter more in ten years than it will tomorrow. Too much CO_2 in the atmosphere will not cause rising seas and widespread drowning for close to a century. It takes years of sewage outfall before shellfish beds in the neighborhood are mortally affected. Fish species shift down the evolutionary scale long after overfishing takes place. Oil from spills in the '60s, buried in sediments, steadily leak hydrocarbons into the water today. Harvesting Antarctic krill will endanger its ecosystem some time in the far-off future when whales regain their abundance, if they do. Time is a different mode in the ocean.

To make decisions on ocean time requires facts about the results of every ocean use. In the past several years, knowledge about ocean systems has burgeoned with amazing speed, filling entire libraries and countless journals. Every day scientists learn more, review each other's writings, concur or question, adding to the richness of available fact. Fifteen years ago, for example, no one knew what happened to oil spilled into the sea. In 1969, the barge *Florida* ruptured its bottom just outside the West Falmouth, Massachusetts, harbor, close to Woods Hole. "The wind from the southwest blew the oil up into Wild River," Howard Sanders, distinguished marine biologist at Woods Hole, remembers. "Then it came back and settled in the sediments of Buzzards Bay." Sanders and/or colleagues have visited the area every year since the spill. In 1983, the oil was still making rainbows in their footprints in the marsh. Sanders' record is the first fourteen-year biography of an oil spill extant. Such knowledge, multiplied in every science, gives us a chance to measure most proposed ocean use against its effects on the ecosystem, immediate or eventual.

We are equipped to make survival decisions about ocean use in many areas. When we do not know enough—mining polymetalic sulfides, a brand new proposition, is an example—we have to put the matter on hold until science can catch up with proposed action.

The United States does not have an ocean policy. What there is exists in bits and pieces and case by case in judicial decisions. Ocean regulation and legislation have not existed long enough to acquire a solid standard; each interpretation builds toward policy. Most often the law's language includes the opposing goals "protect and develop"—and we have so far been unable to choose between

179

them. The masterful ambiguity more or less keeps the peace, leaving us policyless.

The recent extraordinary ocean events—President Reagan's takeover of 1.4 billion ocean acres and his refusal to join most of the world's nations in signing the Law of the Sea—are serious. They force the U.S. to make an ocean policy. Helpful to this effort is a panel of experts, assembled by Eliot Richardson's Citizens for Ocean Law, which will "monitor, analyze and interpret developments in international and national ocean law." Its chairman, Louis Henkin, Columbia University law professor, says the group, mostly academics who were involved in the Law of the Sea negotiations one way or another, hopes "to influence large issues of national policy—mining, fishing, navigation" and aims to make some first recommendations in 1984.

Any U.S. policy must state what use of the EEZ will best serve the public interest. The policy will either bring us closer to putting ourselves first vis-à-vis the sea, or to recognizing the necessity to put the ocean first.

This is the nation's chance to make an historic decision. Possibly we can summon the wisdom to surrender short-term gains that will without doubt destroy the sea. Experience with establishing ocean sanctuaries illustrates the difficulties. The Marine Sanctuary Act, passed by Congress in 1972, authorized the designation of certain specific areas as marine sanctuaries "to protect or restore their conservation, recreation, ecologic or aesthetic values." Since then, this great nation finds just six sites worthy of being sanctuaries under its aegis. The first is the wreck of the Civil War ironclad U.S.S. *Monitor* off North Carolina; the next a part of a coral reef in the Florida Keys. Four more are under consideration. The effort to make Georges Bank, famed fish breeding grounds, a sanctuary failed due to protests from oil prospectors. Another possibility, Sapelo Island off Georgia, did not make it because of local objection to the resultant loss of tax revenue; only a reef 18 miles to the east was approved. The national direction now, a spokesman says, is toward smaller, noncontroversial sites. Considering what we have to save, the sanctuary experience is hardly a proud record.

The National Oceanic and Atmospheric Administration, NOAA, is "the only federal ocean organization," John Byrne, its administrator, says. Ocean-connected functions were scattered throughout the government when he arrived, Byrne tells a visitor, but he has now brought them together in NOAA, part of the U.S. Department of Commerce. A cheerful oceanographer from Oregon State University, formerly at the National Science Foundation, Byrne is well aware of conflicting ocean uses. "I'm not sure we're capable of a national policy for the ocean," he says. "That's the trouble with the democratic process." In mid-'83, Byrne announced a Year of the Ocean to start on March 10, 1984, first anniversary of the acquisition of the billion acres in the sea around us. He wants the Year to "develop an ocean constituency, to emphasize the private sector, including the creation of new industries, and to stir up appreciation of the ocean. Its theme—stewardship of the EEZ."

Byrne assembled "all the ocean-smart people in Washington" to get the Year under way. Chief planners were assorted ocean businessmen, among them, the president of two subsidiaries of a defense contracting firm, the president of a trade association for ocean industries—oil, gas, offshore drilling rigs—the publisher of a magazine and books on sea technology. To run the Year, raise funds, manage publicity, they set up a private nonprofit foundation.

Shock waves reverberated through the environment-minded community. Christopher Roosevelt, lawyer and sea buff, is president of the 70,000-member Oceanic Society which publishes *Oceans* and is the lone national voluntary organization specifically and solely devoted to protection of the sea. Roosevelt wrote Byrne a no-nonsense query concerning the absence of environmentalists in the Year's organization. Byrne's reply did nothing to assuage the impression that the Year was an ocean developer's public relations

181

dream come true. By the time these words are published the Year should be well under way, its impact known. Like most plants, its roots suggest the flowering.

Response to the dramatic events of 1983 is energetic. Within it, the organization of the Year is a small signal, the informative cry of a gull that tells you where the fish are. It need not necessarily dominate what happens next, but the first signs suggest that U.S. action will fit right in with the Year.

"Federal ocean policies are so complex and political that the U.S. must have what amounts to an ocean 'czar,' " states John Botzum, editor of the Nautilus Press, from which newsletters circulate shoptalk in ocean, coast, and climate circles. The czar should "preside over a coordinating body which will be development-oriented rather than science-oriented," Botzum says. Three contenders compete for the throne. There are hints of which way the groups, if crowned, would proceed.

The Ocean Policy Roundtable, put together by the Woods Hole Oceanographic Institution, is a nongovernmental, foundation-financed trial run with a catchall agenda, including almost every foreseeable EEZ use and conflict—except the possibility of its destruction. Discussion plans were put together by Robert Knecht, an old hand at such matters, having steered Coastal Zone Management through the shoals of its first conflict-ridden years. Chairman of the Roundtable is a former senior government relations advisor to the Exxon Corporation; members are a neat balance of Woods Hole executives, outside academics, a category known as "users"—a representative of Gulf Oil, of Sea-Alaska Products Inc.—a foundation president, and none other than czar-proponent Botzum.

The U.S. itself moves to create an official ocean policy commission. An internecine battle for the honor rages between the existing president-appointed National Advisory Committee on Oceans and Atmosphere, NACOA, which claims that ocean policy is within its mandate, and an entirely new group to be created by act of

182

Congress. The Act passed the House in 1983. If it becomes law, it would establish a commission to create ocean law and policy. It is said that the Senate prefers NACOA for the job, having input into NACOA appointments through the Reagan White House.

At this early writing it seems unimportant which of the three contenders, or others which may appear, wins the responsibility of setting the United States' policy for its ocean. They seem clones of each other in membership and intent. Everywhere there are statements for more uses of the ocean, more fishing, dumping, mining, more digging for oil and gas and for the newly discovered sulfides. No group appears any more thoughtful, innovative, or daring than any other, and these characteristics are less than prominent among them. Mediocrity is the common denominator. The proposed U.S. law for a blue-ribbon commission says the central ocean challenge is "the continued leadership of the United States in the sea for the coming decades."

The meaning of this goal is to get the nation out of its self-inflicted isolation from the world's Law of the Sea and back into the international ocean power game. It could also mean that the U.S. can exercise a different kind of ocean leadership, leadership for survival. The U.S. is equipped to treat the ocean with uncompromising care. It can afford to sacrifice ocean-generated wealth for an ocean that encourages life into the future.

The ocean is a world body. Only world agreement can rescue it. But the move has to start somewhere. It should start here.

The nation on its own initiative in 1983 took over the millions of ocean acres it calls the Exclusive Economic Zone. Many other nations also acquired the part of the ocean adjacent to their land, as agreed by the Law of the Sea. This is one of those rare moments in history to be recognized as a time to move out of traditional patterns. All over the world, the EEZ can be the vehicle for unprecedented action.

The U.S. must create a mandate by which to guard the ocean from harm. To lead it requires men who have the quality of intellect and high purpose such as our remarkable Founding Fathers. Nothing less will qualify to do battle to save the ocean. With such men as these in charge, the U.S. can design a plan for the EEZ which will arouse the nation and the world, a plan dedicated to a functioning sea. The 1.4 billion EEZ acres will be used exclusively to protect sea systems. Every proposed use will be measured against this rigid standard. Compromise, tool of democratic political life, cannot be tolerated in the water. If the goal is, as intended, a viable ocean long into the future, we cannot afford even the slightest further damage to any one of its parts.

The burden of proof that a proposed use of the sea will, indeed, be benign, must shift to the user. Presently, it is in the lap of government which routinely passes it to concerned citizens. Efforts to evaluate by bureaucracies, commissioners, even judges are virtually impossible, given the amount of information—scientific, economic, local, state, and federal—that piles up and can obscure the issue or the fatal flaw. Government bodies or individuals are expected not only to analyze the effects of use but to compare them with alternatives, heaping the required study even higher. Additionally, to issue a fair judgment, they must be able to ignore political pressure, a difficult assignment.

A proposed use of the sea is familiar to the user, or it should become familiar. The user can best probe its effects, provide relevant data, evaluate long-term impact. This shift of burden of proof is practical and achievable. More important, it lends dignity and importance, now nonexistent, to using the ocean. Each citizen who would use the sea must use it for his own *and* the general good. And that is easily defined as what is good for the ocean.

Who will judge? As the Congress considers a blue-ribbon panel for the ocean, let it be true blue. The U.S. is rich in scientists and scholars of achievement, wise men, men of intellect, independent of the industrial and government hierarchy. Such men as these should constitute the U.S. government's Ocean Commission.

We will learn to get along without ocean resources which

cannot be safely harvested, oil from the OCS, fish moving toward extinction. We will get along without putting waste in the ocean when we learn that no waste is safe to be thus deposited. The more we have to learn about our proposed ocean use in order to evaluate it, the more we will willingly if not eagerly desist from any one added act of degeneration.

Given the temper of the times, the realist holds few illusions that such a standard for ocean use will be easy or even possible to achieve. It goes against the conventional custom of ocean use in the 1980s in almost all its dimensions. It attacks many traditional ocean freedoms, not for the sake of attacking or for a naive fantasy of a better world, but because our ocean actions, separately and together, have brought about an ocean that threatens us with a rapid decline of the quality of life until life will no longer survive.

There is not one doubt that the reversal of mind required to put the ocean first is our chance to turn the tide, perhaps the last chance. Whatever we must give up to do it, it is worthwhile. The U.S. could boldly lead the nations of the earth to combat Neptune's fearful revenge, freeing the ocean to support life as we enter the worlds of tomorrow.

Bibliography

1. TO RISK THE SEA
Pages 5 to 15.

Albion, Robert G.; William Baker; and Benjamin Labaree. *New England and the Sea*. Middletown, CT: Wesleyan University Press, 1972.

Ballard, Robert D. "Notes on a Major Oceanographic Find." *Oceanus*, summer, 1977.

Barney, Gerald. *Global 2000 Report to the President: Volume 2, The Technical Report*. Washington, DC: U.S. Government Printing Office, 1980.

Beazley, C. Raymond. *Prince Henry the Navigator: The Hero of Portugal and of Modern Discovery*. New York: G. P. Putnam's Sons, 1911.

Bullfinch, Thomas. *The Age of Fable*. New York: New American Library, 1962.

Carse, Robert. *The Seafarers: A History of Maritime America, 1620–1820*. New York, Evanston, IL, London: Harper & Row, Publishers, 1964.

Carson, Rachel L. *The Sea Around Us*. New York: Oxford University Press, 1951.

Cloud, Preston. "Beyond Plate Tectonics." *American Scientist*, July/August, 1980.

Crombie, A. C. *Medieval and Early Modern Science*. Cambridge, MA: Harvard University Press, 1967.

Deacon, Margaret. *Scientists and the Sea 1650–1900*. London: Academic Press, 1971.

Dickson, David. "Radioactive Seaweed Stirs U.K. Low-Level Waste Fight." *Science*, January 6, 1984.

Gross, M. Grant. *Oceanography: A View of the Earth*, 3d edition. Englewood Cliffs, NJ: Prentice Hall, Inc., 1982.

Guberlet, Muriel L. *Explorers of the Sea*. New York: Ronald Press Company, 1964.

Hamilton, Edith. *Mythology*. New York: New American Library, 1942.

Mather, Kirtley F., and Shirley L. Mason. *A Source Book in Geology 1400–1900*. Cambridge, MA : Harvard University Press, 1939.

Menard, H. William. "Anatomy of an Expedition." In Menard, H. W., and J. L. Scheiber, eds., 1976.

Menard, H. William, and Jane L. Scheiber, eds. *Oceans—Our Continuing Frontier.* Del Mar, CA: Publisher's Inc., 1976.

Outhwaite, Leonard. *Unrolling the Map.* New York: John Day Co., 1972 edition.

Parry, J. H. *The Discovery of the Sea.* Berkeley: University of California Press, 1981.

Powledge, Fred. *Water.* New York: Farrar, Straus & Giroux, 1982.

Sanders, John E. *Principles of Physical Geology.* New York: John Wiley & Sons, 1981.

Sarton, George. A *History of Science.* Cambridge, MA: Harvard University Press, 1939.

——. *Six Wings: Men of Science in the Renaissance.* Bloomington: Indiana University Press, 1957.

Schell, Jonathan. "Reflections (Nuclear Arms—Part 1)." *The New Yorker,* January 2, 1984.

Schopf, Thomas J. M. *Paleoceanography.* Cambridge, MA: Harvard University Press, 1980.

Shepard, Francis P. *Geological Oceanography.* New York: Crane, Russak & Company, Inc., 1977.

Wertenbaker, William. "The Floor of the Sea." In Menard, W. H., and J. L. Scheiber, eds., 1976.

——. *The Floor of the Sea.* Boston, Toronto: Little, Brown & Company, 1974.

Weyl, Peter K. *Oceanography.* New York: John Wiley & Sons, Inc., 1970.

2. THE SALMON LEGACY
Pages 17 to 27.

American Museum of Natural History. *Ice Age Art.* New York: Museum publication, 1978.

Association of Scottish District Salmon Fishery Boards. *Salmon Fisheries of Scotland.* Farnham, England: Fishing News Books, Ltd., 1977.

Bewick, Thomas. A *Memoir of Thomas Bewick Written by Himself.* Edited by Montague Weekly. London: Cresset Press, 1961.

Copes, Parzival. "The Law of the Sea Treaty and Management of Anadromous Fish Stocks." *Ocean Development and International Law* 4:3, 1977.

Daye, Peter G. "The Impact of Acid Precipitation on the Physiology and Toxicology of Fish." In International Atlantic Salmon Foundation, 1981.

Ehrlich, Paul and Anne. *Extinction*. New York: Random House, 1981.

Gorham, Eville. "Biological Options." In International Atlantic Salmon Foundation, 1981.

Haines, Terry A. "Effect of Acid Rain on Atlantic Salmon Rivers and Restoration Efforts in the United States." In International Atlantic Salmon Foundation, 1981.

Idyll, Clarence P. *The Sea Against Hunger*. New York: Thomas Y. Crowell, 1978.

International Atlantic Salmon Foundation. Edited by Lee Sochasky. *Acid Rain and the Atlantic Salmon*. New York: International Atlantic Salmon Foundation, 1981.

Johnson, Phillip. "Salmon Ranching." *Oceans*, January, 1982.

Lennon, Robert E. "Bringing the Atlantic Salmon Back." *The Environmental Journal*, August, 1976.

Levinge, Sir Richard. "A General Review of the State of the Salmon Fisheries of the North Atlantic." In Went, A. E. J., 1980.

Muniz, Ivar P. "Acidification and the Norwegian Salmon." In International Atlantic Salmon Foundation, 1981.

Radcliffe, William. *Fishing from the Earliest Times*. New York: Burt Franklin, 1969.

"Salmon Return to Connecticut River." Environmental Defense Fund Letter, July 8, 1980.

Sherman, Kenneth; C. Jones; L. Sullivan; P. Berrien; and L. Ejsymont. "Congruent Shifts in Sand Eel Abundance in Western and Eastern North Atlantic Ecosystems." *Nature*, June 11, 1981.

United Nations Environment Programme, *Marine Living Resources*. United Nations Environment Programme, 1980.

"Washington Roundup." *Chemical and Engineering News*, January 25, 1982.

Waterman, Charles F. *Fishing in America*. New York: Holt, Rinehart & Winston, 1975.

Went, Arthur Edward James. *Atlantic Salmon: Its Future*. Farnham, England: Fishing News Books, Ltd., 1980.

Williams, R. O. M. "The Angler's Viewpoint." In Went, A. E. J., 1980.

3. IMPRUDENT PREDATORS
Pages 29 to 41.

Ahlstrom, Elbert A., and John Radovich. "Management of the Pacific Sardine." In Benson, Norman G., ed., 1970.

Albion, Robert G.; William Baker; and Benjamin Labaree. *New England and the Sea*. Middletown, CT: Wesleyan University Press, 1972.

Benson, Norman G., ed. *A Century of Fisheries in North America*. Washington, DC: American Fisheries Society, 1970.

Brown, Lester R. *The Twenty-Ninth Day*. New York: W. W. Norton and Co., Inc., 1978.

Byrne, Dr. John V. before the Speech Marine Recreational Fisheries Symposium, Fort Lauderdale, FL, May 10, 1982. Washington, DC: National Oceanographic and Atmospheric Administration, May 1982.

Christy, Francis T., Jr., and Anthony Scott. *The Common Wealth in Ocean Fisheries*. Baltimore and London: Johns Hopkins Press, 1965.

Council of Environmental Quality. *Environmental Trends*. Washington DC: U.S. Government Printing Office, July 1981.

Dickie, L. M. "Problems in Prediction." *Oceanus*, winter, 1975.

Encyclopaedia Britannica (14th ed.). Entries on "Fish," "Fishing," and "Sir Wm. Monson." New York: Encyclopaedia Britannica, Inc., 1929.

Graham, Avery, and W. Roy Siegfried. "Food Gatherers Along South Africa's Seashore." *Oceans*, July/August, 1980.

Hagan, Patti. "The Singular Krill." *New York Times Magazine*, March 9, 1975.

Hamilton, Edith, and Huntington Cairns, eds. *The Collected Dialogues of Plato*. New York: Bollingen Foundation, 1961.

Hennemuth, Richard C. "Marine Fisheries: Food for the Future?" *Oceanus*, spring, 1979.

Jensen, Albert C. *The Cod—The Uncommon History of a Common Fish and Its Impact on American Life from Viking Times to the Present*. New York: Thomas Y. Crowell Co., 1972.

"Mass. Fishing, a Resource Disaster." *Environmental Resource*, no date.

McHugh, J. I., and E. H. Ahlstrom. "Is the Pacific Sardine Disappearing?" *Scientific Monthly*, June, 1951.

Meltzer, Michael. *The World of the Small Commercial Fisherman*. New York: Dover Publications, 1980.

Murphy, Garth I. "Oceanography and Variations in the Pacific Sardine Population." *California Cooperative Oceanic Fisheries Investigations*. Reports, July 1, 1959 to June 30, 1960.

National Advisory Council on Oceans and Atmosphere. "National Ocean Goals and Objectives for the 1980's." *Ocean Services for the Nation*, January, 1980.

National Marine Fisheries Service. *Fisheries of the United States, 1980*. Washington, DC: National Oceanographic and Atmospheric Administration, April, 1981.

———. *Marine Recreational Fisheries Highlights*, December 10, 1981.

Pontecorvo, Giulio; Maurice Wilkinson; Ronald Anderson; Michael Holdowsky. "Contribution of the Ocean Sector to the United States Economy." *Science*, May 30, 1980.

Robinson, M. A., and Adele Crispoldi. "Trends in World Fisheries." *Oceanus*, winter, 1975.

Sanders, John E. *Principles of Physical Geology*. New York: John Wiley & Sons, 1981.

Smith, J. A., and W. D. Ross, eds. *The Works of Aristotle: Volume 4, Historia Animalium*. Oxford: Clarendon Press, 1910.

Smith, W. G. "Sand Lance Larvae Abundance; Atlantic Herring Larvae Disappearance," *Coastal Oceanography and Climatology News* 4:2, 1982.

Smith, W. G.; D. G. McMillan; and A. Wells. *The Distribution and Abundance of Atlantic Herring Larvae in the Gulf of Maine Region as Determined from MARMAP Surveys During Autumn and Winter, 1980–1981*. Sandy Hook, NJ: National Oceanographic and Atmospheric Administration, September, 1981.

Steinbeck, John. *Cannery Row*. New York: Penguin Books, 1981.

Storer, James A., and Nancy Bockstael. "LOS and the Fisheries," *Oceanus*, winter, 1975.

"Tanker Pollution." Ocean World Special Report. *Ocean Reporter*, April/May, 1978.

United Nations Environmental Programme. *Marine Living Resources*. 1980.

U.S. Census Bureau. *1970 Census Report*. Washington, DC: U.S. Government Printing Office, 1971.

U.S. Congress. Public Law 94-265, Fishery Conservation and Management Act (Magnuson Act), April 13, 1976.

U.S. Department of Commerce. *U.S. Ocean Policy in the 1970's: Status and Issues*. Washington DC: U.S. Department of Commerce, October, 1978.

U.S. Department of Commerce, National Oceanic and Atmospheric Administration. *Report to the Congress on Ocean Pollution, Overfishing, and Offshore Development—July 1975 through September 1976*. November, 1977.

Walton, Izaak. *The Compleat Angler*. London: Chiswick Press, 1903.

Wheeler, Alwyne. *Fishes of the World*. New York: Macmillan Publishing Co., Inc., 1975.

4. A SELECTION OF POISONS
Pages 43 to 57.

Adler, Jerry. "How Fragile Is the Ocean." *National Wildlife*, April/May, 1982.

Backus, R. *Georges Bank*. Geneva: Coastal Research Center, World Health Organization (in preparation).

Barney, Gerald O. *Global 2000 Report to the President*. Washington, DC: U.S. Government Printing Office, 1980.

Blumer, Max. "Oil Contamination and the Living Resources in the Sea." In Ruivo, M., ed., 1972.

Bulloch, David. "Plankton Productivity of the Sea." *Underwater Naturalist*, summer, 1982.

Carefoot, Thomas. *Pacific Seashores—A Guide to Intertidal Ecology*. Seattle: University of Washington Press, 1977.

Council on Environmental Quality. *Global Energy Futures and the Carbon Dioxide Problem*. Washington, DC: Council on Environmental Quality, January, 1981.

Global Future: Time to Act: Report to the President on Global Resources, Environment and Population. Washington, DC: Council on Environmental Quality, January, 1981.

Davis, Charles C. *The Marine and Fresh-Water Plankton*. Michigan State University Press, 1955.

Diemer, F. P., et al., eds. *Advanced Concepts in Ocean Measurement for Marine Biology*. Charleston: University of South Carolina Press, 1980.

Duggan, James, and Susan Barker. "New Jersey Phytoplankton." *Underwater Naturalist*, summer, 1982.

"Dwindling Catches Plague Shrimpers in Carolinas." *New York Times*, November 2, 1982.

Edwards, Robert L. "Middle Atlantic Fisheries: Recent Changes in Populations and Outlook." In M. Grant Gross, ed., 1976.

Encyclopaedia Britannica (14th ed.). Entry on "Plankton." New York: Encyclopaedia Britannica, Inc., 1929.

Fisher, Nicholas S. "Chlorinated Hydrocarbons Pollutants and Photosynthesis of Marine Phytoplankton: A Reassessment." *Science*, August 8, 1975.

———. "North Sea Phytoplankton." *Nature*, January 15, 1976.

———. "On the Differential Sensitivity of Estuarine and Open-Ocean Diatoms to Exotic Chemical Stress." *American Naturalist*, September, 1977.

Gross, M. Grant, ed. *Middle Atlantic Continental Shelf and the New York Bight*. Lawrence, KS: Allen Press, Inc., 1976.

Gross, M. Grant. "Waste Sources and Effects." In *Middle Atlantic Continental Shelf and the New York Bight*. Gross, M. Grant, ed., 1976.

Grove, Noel. "Superspill—Black Day for Brittany." *National Geographic*, July, 1978.

Guillard, R. L., and Lynda S. Murphy. "Comparative Environmental Physiology of Marine Phytoplankton: Responses to Oligotrophic Waters" (research proposal to the National Science Foundation).

Hanley, Robert. "Jersey, Citing PCB Levels, Urges Limit on Eating Five Kinds of Fish." *New York Times*, December 14, 1982.

192

Hess, Wilmot H. *The Amoco Cadiz Oil Spill.* Washington, DC: U.S. Government Printing Office, 1978.

Howarth, Robert W. "Oil and Fish: Can They Co-exist?" In Jackson, Thomas C., and Diana Reische, eds., 1981.

————. "Potential Effects of Petroleum on the Biotic Resources of Georges Bank." In Backus, R., ed. (in preparation).

————. "Statement Before the Committee on Commerce, Science and Transportation." Washington, DC: U.S. Senate, December 5, 1979.

Jackson, Thomas C., and Diana Reische, eds. *Coast Alert.* San Francisco: Friends of the Earth, 1981.

Klutznick, (Commerce Secretary) Philip M. *Report to the Congress on Ocean Pollution and Offshore Development.* Washington, DC: Department of Commerce, 1978.

Kumpf, Herman E. *Economic Impact of the Effects of Pollution on the Coastal Fisheries of the Atlantic and Gulf of Mexico Regions of the U.S.A.* Rome: United Nations Food and Agricultural Organization, 1977.

Luepke, N. P., ed. *Monitoring Environmental Materials and Speciman Banking.* The Hague: Martinas Nijhoff, 1979.

Mayer, Garry, ed. *Ecological Stress in the N.Y. Bight.* Columbia: University of South Carolina Press, 1982.

Morson, Barbara. "The Argo Merchant Oil Spill: Impact on Birds and Mammals." *Proceedings of the Conference of Ecological Impact of Oil Spills.* Washington, DC: American Institute of Biological Sciences, June, 1978.

Murphy, Lynda; Robert L. Guillard; and Jerome Gavis. "Evolution of Resistant Phytoplankton Strains Through Exposure to Marine Pollutants." In Mayer, G., ed., 1982.

National Academy of Sciences. *Disposal in the Marine Environment: An Oceanographic Assessment.* Study for the Environmental Protection Agency. Washington, DC: National Academy of Sciences, 1976.

————. *Petroleum in the Marine Environment.* Washington DC: National Academy of Sciences, 1975.

National Oceanographic and Atmospheric Administration. *Assessment Report on the Effects of Waste Dumping in 106-Mile Ocean Waste Disposal Site.* Boulder, CO: National Oceanographic and Atmospheric Administration, May, 1981.

Ortner, Peter B., and Lynda S. Murphy. *Biological Effects of a Dump at 106-Mile Site.* Washington, DC: National Oceanographic and Atmospheric Administration, May, 1981.

Pearce, John B. "The Effect of Solid Waste Disposal on Benthic Communities in the New York Bight." In Ruivo, M., ed., 1972.

193

————. "The Effects of Pollution and the Need for Long-Term Monitoring," *Helgolander Weeresuntersuchungen* 34:2, 1980.

————. "Trace Metals in Living Resources." In Luepke, N.P., ed., 1979.

————, and Oillington Lockwood. "Monitoring the Health of the Northeast Continental Shelf: An Update." *Bulletin of the Coastal Society*, April/August, 1981.

Raymont, John E. G. *Plankton and Productivity of the Oceans*. Oxford, NY: Pergamon Press, c. 1963.

Reid, Philip C. "Large Scale Changes in North Sea Phytoplankton." *Nature*, September 18, 1975.

Reid, Robert N., and David J. Radosh. "Benthic Macrofaunal Recovery After the 1976 Hypoxia off New Jersey." *Coastal Oceanography and Climatology News*, spring, 1979.

Ruivo, Mario, ed. *Marine Pollution and Sea Life*. London: Fishing News (Books) Ltd., 1972.

Russell, Dick. "The Venerable Striped Bass—An Endangered Species." *The Amicus Journal*, fall, 1982.

Shanley, Andrew. "Challenge to American Coast Puts Island Waters at Center." *Vineyard Gazette*, September 10, 1982.

Sherman, John W. "An Overview of Remote Sensing Oceanography in the United States." *Twelfth International Symposium on Remote Sensing of Environment*. Ann Arbor: Environmental Research Institute of Michigan, April, 1978.

Sherman, Kenneth. "MARMAP, a Fisheries Ecosystem Study in the Northwest Atlantic." In Diemer, F.P., ed., 1980.

Sindermann, Carl J. "Environmental Stress in Oceanic Bivalve Mollusc Populations." *Proceedings of the National Shellfish Association* 69, 1979.

————. "Fish and Environmental Impacts." Proceedings, Fourth Congress of European Icthyologists, Hamburg, West Germany, September, 1982.

————. "Fish and Fisheries—Effects of Coastal Pollution on Fish and Fisheries—With Particular Reference to the Middle Atlantic Bight." In Gross, M. Grant, ed., 1976.

————. "Pollution Associated Diseases and Abnormalities of Fish and Shellfish." *Fishery Bulletin* 16:4, 1979.

————. "Some Biological Indicators of Marine Environmental Degradation." *Washington Journal of the Academy of Sciences* 62:2, 1972.

Steimle, Frank W., and Carl J. Sindermann. "Review of Oxygen Depletion and Associated Mass Mortalities of Shellfish in the Middle Atlantic Bight in 1976." *Marine Fisheries Review* 40:12, 1978.

Stout, Virginia F.; Clifford R. Houle; and F. Lee Beezhold. "A Survey of Chlorinated Hydrocarbons Residues in Menhaden Fishery Products." *Marine Fisheries Review* 43:3, 1981.

"Stripper Research yields Ominoius Results." *Right Rigger*, June, 1982.

Teal, John M., and Robert W. Howarth. "Oil Spill Studies: A Review of Ecological Effects." *Environmental Management* (in press).

Tucker, Anthony. *The Toxic Metals.* London: Earth Island Limited, 1972.

United Nations Environmental Programme. *The Health of the Oceans.* Nairobi, Kenya: United Nations Environmental Programme Regional Seas Reports and Studies, No. 16, 1982.

United Nations Food and Agricultural Organization. *Pollution.* Rome: United Nations Food and Agricultural Organization, 1971.

Vernberg, Winona B.; Frederick P. Thurberg; Anthony Calabrese; and F. John Vernberg; eds. *Marine Pollution: Functional Responses.* New York: Academic Press, 1979.

Wildlife Management Institute. *Wildlife, the Environmental Barometer.* Washington, DC: U.S. Department of the Interior, no date.

5. OIL ON THE LOOSE
Pages 59 to 75.

"Alaska Governor Cleared in Oil Lease Inquiry." *New York Times*, October 1, 1983.

Allen, David, et al. "Effects on Commercial Fishing of Petroleum Development off the Northeastern United States." *Woods Hole Oceanographic Institution*, April, 1974.

American Petroleum Institute. *Basic Petroleum Data Book.* Vol. III, no. 1. Washington, DC: American Petroleum Institute, January, 1983.

———. *Facts About Oil.* Washington, DC: American Petroleum Institute, no date.

———. *The Why and How of Undersea Drilling.* Washington, DC: American Petroleum Institute, no date.

Backus, R. *Georges Bank.* Geneva: Coastal Research Center, World Health Organization (in preparation).

Bates, Sarah. "The Struggle for Georges Bank." In McLeod, G. C., and J. H. Prescott, eds., 1982.

Becker, Jasper. "North Sea Still Suffering." *Nature*, March 24, 1983.

Beinecke, Frances. "Comments on Sale No. 57, Proposed Notice of Sale and Consistency Determination." Natural Resources Defense Council, December, 1982.

Borgese, Elizabeth Mann, and Norton Ginsburg, eds. *Ocean Yearbook 2.* Chicago and London: University of Chicago Press, 1980.

Conant, Melvin A. "The Call of the Arctic." *Oceanus*, winter 1982/83.

Connor, Michael S., and Robert W. Howarth. *Potential Effects of Oil Production on Georges Bank Communities: A Review of the Draft EIS for the OCS Oil and Gas Lease Sale No. 42*. Technical Report Prepared for the U.S. Department of Commerce, NOAA, and WHOI, January, 1977.

"The Costly Hunt for Arctic Oil." *New York Times*, June 17, 1980.

Council on Environmental Quality. *Environmental Trends*. Washington, DC: Council on Environmental Quality, July, 1981.

————. *OCS Oil and Gas*. Washington, DC: Council on Environmental Quality, April, 1974.

Dannenberger, Elmer P. *Outer Continental Shelf Oil and Gas Blowouts*. Washington, DC: U.S. Department of the Interior Geological Survey, 1980.

Dolton, G. L., et al. "Estimates of Undiscovered Recoverable Conventional Resources of Oil and Gas in the U.S." *Geological Survey* 860. Alexandria, Virginia, 1981.

Drew, Christopher. "The Sorrows of a 'Superport'—Too Much, Too Late." *New York Times*, January 30, 1983.

Exxon. *Deepwater Capabilities*. Houston, TX: Exxon Production Research Co., 1976.

————. *Submerged Production System*. Houston, TX: Exxon Production Research Company, no date.

Fisher, William L. "How Much Oil Remains?" *Scope*, November/December, 1981.

Gaskell, T. F., and S. J. R. Simpson. "Oil: Two Billion DC—AD Two Thousand." In Borgese, E. M., and N. Ginsburg, eds., 1980.

Harwood, Michael. "Oil and Water." *Harpers*, September, 1978.

Hess, Wilmot, ed. *The Amoco Cadiz Oil Spill*. Washington, DC: U.S. Department of Commerce, April, 1978.

Hildreth, Richard G., and Ralph W. Johnson. *Ocean and Coastal Law*. Englewood Cliffs, NJ: Prentice Hall, Inc., 1983.

Hooper, Craig H., ed. *The Ixtoc 1 Oil Spill, The Federal Scientific Response*. Boulder, CO: U.S. Department of Commerce, December, 1981.

Howarth, Robert W. "Potential Impacts of Petroleum on the Biotic Resources of Georges Bank." In Backus, R. (in preparation).

Interagency Committee on Ocean Pollution Research, Development and Monitoring. *Marine Oil Pollution: Federal Program Review*. Washington, DC: U.S. Department of Commerce, April, 1981.

————. *National Marine Pollution Program Plan, 1981–1985*. Washington DC: U.S. Department of Commerce, September, 1981.

Johnson, John H. "Presence and Sources of Oil in the Sediment and Benthic Community Surrounding the Ekofisk Field After the Blowout at Bravo." Northbrook, IL: NALCO Environmental Services, 1977.

196

Kitlutsisti, Nunam, ed. *The Issue Is Survival.* Mt. Village, AK: Coastal Resource Service Area Board, no date.

Kumpf, Herman E. *Economic Impact of the Effects of Pollution on the Coastal Fisheries of the Atlantic and Gulf of Mexico.* Rome: United Nations Food and Agricultural Organization, 1977.

Levy, Walter J. *Oil Strategy and Politics 1941–1981.* Boulder, CO: Westview Press, 1982.

"Liberian Ships and Oil Spills." *New York Times,* January 2, 1977.

"LOOP's Last Link." *Texaco Star,* 1982.

McLeod, Guy C., and John H. Prescott, eds. *Georges Banks: Past, Present and Future of a Marine Environment.* Boulder, CO: Westview Press, 1982.

Murphy, Lynda S., and Peter R. Hoar. "Effect of Pollutants on Marine Phytoplankton at 106 Mile Site." In National Oceanographic and Atmospheric Administration, 1981.

National Academy of Sciences. *Petroleum in the Marine Environment.* Washington, DC: National Academy of Sciences, 1975.

National Oceanographic and Atmospheric Administration. *Assessment Report on the Effects of Waste Dumping in 106-Mile Ocean Waste Disposal Site.* Boulder, CO: National Oceanographic and Atmospheric Administration, May, 1981.

Natural Resources Defense Council, Inc. *Offshore Oil Leasing.* New York: Natural Resources Defense Council, 1980.

Not Man Apart. "Persian Gulf, a Casualty of War." San Francisco: Friends of the Earth, October, 1983.

Richardson, Elliot L. "Prevention of Vessel-Source Pollution—An Attainable Goal." *Oceans,* March/April and May/June, 1980.

"The Sorrows of a Superport." *New York Times,* January 30, 1983.

"Tanker Pollution." Ocean World Special Report. *Ocean Reporter,* April/May, 1978.

United Nations Environment Programme. *The Health of the Oceans.* Nairobi, Kenya: United Nations Environment Programme Regional Seas and Studies, No. 16, 1982.

U.S. Coast Guard. Navigation and Vessel Inspection Circular 1-81. Washington, DC: U.S. Department of Transportation, 1981.

U.S. Court of Appeals. *Commonwealth of Massachusetts and Conservation Law Foundation of New England vs. Cecil Andrus, Secretary, with Atlantic Richfield,* brief for the federal appellants.

———, First Circuit. Reply Brief for the Federal Appellants. No. 78-1036 and 78-1037. *Massachusetts et al., and Conservation Law Foundation of New England et al., vs. Andrus et al., and Atlantic Richfield et al.,* February 28, 1978.

U.S. Court of Appeals for District of Columbia Circuit. *State of California et al., vs. James G. Watt, Secretary of the Interior.* No. 82-1822 thru 82–1826.

197

————. *State of California, California Coastal Communities et al., vs. James Watt, Secretary of the Interior and American Petroleum Institute, Respondents, 1981.* No. 80-1894.

U.S. Department of Energy, Energy Information Administration. *1981 Annual Report to Congress,* vol. 2. Washington, DC: U.S. Department of Energy, May, 1982.

————. *7th Ocean Energy Conference, Expanded Abstracts.* Washington, DC: U.S. Department of Energy, June, 1980.

U.S. Department of the Interior. "Approval of 5-Year OCS Oil and Gas Leasing Program Announced." News release. Washington, DC: U.S. Department of the Interior, July 21, 1982.

————. *Final Environmental Impact Statement, February 1982—Proposed Outer Continental Shelf Oil and Gas Lease Sale—Norton Sound.* Washington, DC: U.S. Department of the Interior, 1982.

————. "Secretarial Issue Document for Tentative Proposed Final 5-Year OCS Leasing Program." *Department of the Interior,* March 1, 1982.

U.S. Environmental Protection Agency. *Oil Spills.* Washington, DC: U.S. Environmental Protection Agency, 1979.

————. *Oil Spills and Spills of Hazardous Substances.* Washington, DC: U.S. Environmental Protection Agency, March, 1977.

"U.S. Judge Blocks Sale of Georges Bank Oil Leases." *New York Times,* March 29, 1983.

Watt, (Interior Secretary) James. *Statement on Norton Basin Offshore Lease Offering.* Washington, DC: U.S. Department of the Interior, January 25, 1983.

Weicker, (Senator) Lowell. "Big Oil Lowers the Bit on New England's Best Fisheries." *Sport Diver,* March/April, 1980.

————. "Purpose: To Provide for Review of Secretary Watt's 5-Year OCS Leasing Program." *Congressional Record,* September 29, 1982.

6. THE SEA AS A SINK
Pages 77 to 95.

Cameron, Francis X. "Radioactive Waste Disposal Facility Siting: Impact on Coastal Areas." *Coastal Society Bulletin,* April-August, 1981.

Carter, Luther J. "Navy Considers Scuttling Old Subs." *Science,* September 26, 1980.

Carter, Luther J. "The Radwaste Paradox." *Science.* January 7, 1983.

Comptroller General of the United States. *The Problem of Disposing of Nuclear*

Low-Level Waste: Where Do We Go From Here? Washington, DC: General Accounting Office, March 31, 1980.

Cousteau, Jacques-Yves. Letter, no date.

Curtis, Clifton E. "International Moratorium Adopted for Ocean Dumping of Radioactive Waste Despite U.S. Opposition." *Oceans*, May, 1983.

De Camp, L. Sprague. *The Ancient Engineers*. Garden City, NY: Doubleday & Co., 1963.

Dorgan, Michael. "20,000 Rads Under the Sea." *Environmental Action*, April, 1981.

Farrington, John W., et al. "Ocean Dumping." *Oceanus*, winter, 1982–83.

Franz, D. R. "An Historical Perspective on Molluscs in Lower New York Harbor With Emphasis on Oysters." in Mayer, G. F., ed., 1982.

Gofman, John W., M.D. *Radiation and Human Health*. San Francisco: Sierra Club Books, 1981.

Goyal, Sagar M. "Viral Pollution of Marine Environment." *Reviews in Environmental Control*, CRC Press (in press).

————; Charles P. Gerba; and Joseph L. Melnick. "Transferable Drug Resistance in Bacteria of Coastal Canal Water and Sediment." *Water Research* 13, 1979.

Hollister, Charles D. "The Seabed Option." *Oceanus*, winter, 1977.

————; D. Richard Anderson; and G. Ross Heath. "Subsea-Bed Disposal of Nuclear Wastes." *Science*, September 18, 1981.

————; William P. Bishop; and David A. Deese. "Siting Considerations and Political Implications for the Disposal of High Level Nuclear Wastes Beneath the Deep Sea Floor." Paper for Marine Sciences and Ocean Policy Symposium, Santa Barbara University of California, June, 17–20, 1979.

————; B. H. Corliss; and D. R. Anderson. "Submarine Geologic Disposal of Nuclear Waste." *Underground Disposal of Radioactive Wastes*, 1980.

Hughes, J. Donald. *Ecology in Ancient Civilizations*. Albuquerque: University of New Mexico Press, 1975.

Kester, D. R., B. H. Ketchum, and P. K. Park. "Future Prospects of Ocean Dumping." In Ketchum, Bostwick H., et al., eds., 1981.

Ketchum, Bostwick, H.; Dana R. Kester; and P. Kihlo Park; eds. *Ocean Dumping of Industrial Wastes*. New York: Plenum Press, 1981.

Koch, (Mayor) Edward I. Testimony before the Merchant Marine and Fisheries Subcommittee on Oceanography and Subcommittee on Fisheries and Wildlife Conservation and the Environment. *Congressional Record*, March 23, 1982.

Loop, Anne S. *History and Development of Sewage Treatment in New York City*. New York: New York City Department of Health, 1964.

199

Lounsbery, W. J., and L. K. Glover. "Banning Ocean Dumping: So Near But Yet Sofaer." *Coastal Ocean Pollution Assessment News*, 1982.

Mayer, Garry F., ed. *Biological Stress and the New York Bight: Science and Management*. Columbia, SC: Estuarine Research Federation, 1982.

National Academy of Sciences. *Assessing Potential Ocean Pollutants*. Washington, DC: National Academy of Sciences, 1975.

National Advisory Committee on Oceans and Atmosphere. *The Role of the Ocean in a Waste Management Strategy*. Washington, DC: National Advisory Committee on Oceans and Atmosphere, 1981.

U.S. District Court for the District of New Jersey. *National Wildlife Federation and New Jersey State Federation of Sportsmen's Clubs vs. U.S. Environmental Protection Agency*, January 17, 1983.

"Navy's Sub Dump Plan Meets Bold Resistance." *Greenpeace Examiner*, spring, 1983.

New York State Department of Health. *News*, December 28, 1982.

Norman, Colin. "U.S. Considers Ocean Dumping of Radwastes." *Science*, March 5, 1982.

"Nuclear Wastes Leaking on the Ocean Floor." *New York Times*, May 23, 1976.

Ocean Disposal Study Steering Committee. *Disposal in the Marine Environment: An Oceanographic Assessment*. Washington, DC: National Academy of Sciences, 1976.

Oceanic Society. *Disposal of Defueled, Decommissioned Submarines*. Stamford, CT: The Oceanic Society, December 10, 1982.

O'Halloran, Robert L. "Ocean Dumping: Progress Toward a Rational Policy of Dredged Waste Disposal." *Environmental Law*. Chicago: Northwestern School of Law, spring, 1982.

Park, P. K., and Thomas P. O'Connor. "Ocean Dumping Research." In Ketchum, Bostwick H., et al., eds., 1981.

Powledge, Fred. "Life Amidst the Ruins." *The Amicus Journal*, summer, 1982.

Risoli, Susan J. "NOAA, EPA Monitor Radioactive Waste Disposal Site in Massachusetts Bay." *Coastal Ocean Pollution Assessment News* 2:1, 1982.

Sandia National Laboratories. "The Subseabed Disposal Program." *Sandia Technology*, September, 1981.

―――. *Subseabed Disposal Program Plan*. Albuquerque, NM: Sandia National Laboratories, July, 1981.

Shapiro, Fred C. *Radwaste*. New York: Random House, 1981.

Sofaer, Hon. Abraham D. *Opinion in the case of the City of New York vs. the Environmental Protection Agency*; April 14, 1981; August 26, 1981. U.S. District Court of Southern District of New York.

Squires, Donald F. *The Ocean Dumping Quandary—Waste Disposal in the New York Bight*. Albany, NY: State University Press, 1983.

"Swiss to Continue Dumping Radioactive Wastes in Ocean." *New York Times*, May 26, 1983.

U.S. Department of the Navy. *Draft Environmental Impact Statement on the Disposal of Decommissioned, Defueled, Naval Submarines Reactor Plants*. Washington, DC: December, 1982.

U.S. Environmental Protection Agency. *Annual Report to Congress, Jan.–Dec. 1979: On Administration of the Marine Protection, Research, and Sanctuaries Act of 1972*. Washington, DC: Office of Water Programs, May, 1980.

————. *Annual Report to Congress, Jan.–Dec., 1980: On Administration of the Marine Protection, Research and Sanctuaries Act of 1972*. Washington, D.C.: Environmental Protection Agency, December 30, 1981.

7. THE SEA ALSO RISES
Pages 97 to 114.

Baes, Charles F., Jr. "Effects of Ocean Chemistry and Biology on Atmospheric Carbon Dioxide." In Clark, William C., ed., 1982.

Bowen, D. Q. "Rapid Environmental and Climatic Changes." *Nature*, September 16, 1982.

Bretherton, Francis P. "The Problems of Climate Research." *Oceanus*, fall, 1978.

Brewer, Peter G. "Carbon Dioxide and Climate." *Oceanus*, fall, 1978.

————. "Carbon Dioxide and Ocean Chemistry." Washington, DC: U.S. Department of Energy, 1982.

Bryan, Kirk. "The Ocean Heat Balance." *Oceanus*, fall, 1978.

Center for Ocean Management Studies. *Climate and Fisheries*. Kingston: University of Rhode Island Press, 1978.

Clark, William C., ed. *Carbon Dioxide Review 1982*. Oxford, England: Oxford University Press, 1982.

Clark, William C., et al. "The Carbon Dioxide Question: Perspective for 1982." In Clark, William C., 1982.

Council on Environmental Quality. *Global Energy Futures and the Carbon Dioxide Problem*. Washington, DC: U.S. Government Printing Office, January, 1981.

Daniel, Howard. *Man and Climatic Variability*. Geneva: World Meterological Organization, 1980.

Emiliani, Cesare. "Ice Sheets and Ice Melts." *Natural History*, November, 1980.

Etkins, Robert, and Edward S. Epstein. "The Rise of Global Mean Sea Level as an Indication of Climate Change." *Science*, January 15, 1982.

"Evidence Is Found of Warmup Trend." *New York Times*, October 19, 1981.

Flohn, Hermann. "Climate Change and an Ice-Free Arctic Ocean." In Clark, William C., ed., 1982.

Gornitx, V.; S. Lebedeff; and J. Hansen. "Global Sea Level Trend in the Past Century." *Science*, March 26, 1982.

Hoffman, John S. "Contingency Planning for a Hotter Earth." *Directors and Boards*, fall, 1982.

Hoffman, John S., and Michael Barth. "Carbon Dioxide." *The Amicus Journal*, summer, 1983.

Houghton, R. A. et al. "Changes in the Carbon Content of Terrestrial Biota and Soils between 1860 and 1980: A Net Release of CO_2 to the Atmosphere." *Ecological Monographs*, September, 1982.

Kellogg, William W., and Robert Schware. "Society, Science and Climate Change." *Foreign Affairs*, summer, 1982.

Lamb, H. H. *Climate, History and the Modern World*. London and New York: Methuen, 1982.

Massachusetts Institute of Technology. *Inadvertent Climate Modification*. Cambridge, MA, and London: MIT Press, 1971.

McElroy, M. B. "Marine Biological Controls on Atmospheric CO_2 and Climate." *Nature*, March 24, 1983.

McKay, Dr. G. A.; T. R. Allsopp; and J. B. Maxwell. "Lesson from the Past." *Climate and Offshore Energy Resources*, October 21, 1980.

McLean, Dewey M. "Terminal Mesozoic 'Greenhouse': Lessons from the Past." *Science*, August 4, 1978.

National Research Council. *Carbon Dioxide and Climate: A Scientific Assessment*. Washington, DC: National Academy of Sciences, 1979.

Parrot, André. *The Flood and Noah's Ark*. New York: New York Philosophical Library, 1955.

Ponté, Lowell. *The Cooling*. Englewood Cliffs, NJ: Prentice Hall, Inc., 1976.

Revelle, Roger. "Carbon Dioxide and World Climate." *Scientific American*, August, 1982.

———. "Commentary." In Clark, William C.; ed., 1982.

———. "The Oceans and the Carbon Dioxide Problem." *Oceanus*. summer 1983.

Roberts, Walter Orr. "It Is Time to Prepare for Global Climate Changes." Conservation Foundation letter, April, 1983.

Seidel, Stephen, and Dale Keys. *Can We Delay a Greenhouse Warming?* Washington, DC: U.S. Office of Policy and Resources Management, September, 1983.

Simon, Anne W. *The Thin Edge: Coast and Man in Crisis*. New York: Harper & Row, 1978.

Sullivan, Walter. "Earth Said to Be in 'Icehouse.' " *New York Times*, September 20, 1983.

Titus, James G., et al. "Sea-Level Rise Overview Paper." *Sea-Level Rise Conference*. Washington, DC: U.S. Environmental Protection Agency, March, 1983.

U.S. Department of Energy. *The First Detection of CO_2 Effects Workshop Proceedings*. Washington, DC: U.S. Department of Energy, 1982.

U.S. Environmental Protection Agency. Edited by Michael Barth and Jim Titus. *Sea Level Rise to the Year 2100*. Stroudsburg, PA: Hutchinson and Ross, 1984.

Woodwell, George M. "The Carbon Dioxide Question." *Scientific American*, January, 1978.

World Meteorological Organization. *Proceedings on the World Climate Conference*. Geneva: World Meteorological Organization, February, 1971.

8. OCEAN GRAB: MAKING IT LEGAL
Pages 115 to 134.

Armstrong, John M., and Peter C. Ryner. *Ocean Management: A New Perspective*. Ann Arbor, MI: Ann Arbor Science Publishers, Inc., 1981.

Chapman, Stephen. "Underwater Plunder." *The New Republic*, April 21, 1982.

Copes, Parzival. "The Law of the Sea and Management of Anadromous Fish Stocks." *Ocean Development and International Law* 4:3, 1977.

Crane, Kathleen, and Robert Ballard. "The Galapogos Rift at 86 W." *Journal of Geophysical Research*, March 10, 1980.

Curlin, James W. "At Last: A Framework for Modern Ocean Policy." *Marine Technology Society Journal*, June 1980.

Curtis, Clifton. "The Environmental Aspects of Deep Ocean Mining." *Oceanus*, fall, 1982.

———. "In Everyone's Interest—There Must Be a Law for the Sea." *Oceanic Society*, January, 1982.

———. Statement before Subcommittee on Oceanography of the House Committee on Merchant Marine and Fisheries concerning nuclear waste disposal in the oceans, November 20, 1980.

———. Statement before the Subcommittee on Oceanography of House Committee on Merchant Marine and Fisheries concerning U.S. review of draft Law of the Sea, October 22, 1981.

East Pacific Rise Study Group. "Crustal Processes of the Mid-Ocean Ridge." *Science*, July 3, 1981.

Eckert, Ross D. *The Enclosure of Ocean Resources.* Stanford, CA: Hoover Institution Press, 1979.

Encyclopaedia Britannica (14th ed.). Entry on "Grotius, Hugo." New York: Encyclopaedia Britannica, Inc., 1927.

Frank, Richard A. "Jumping Ship." *Foreign Policy,* summer, 1981.

Friedman, Wolfgang. *The Future of the Oceans.* New York: George Braziller, Inc., 1971.

Fye, Paul M. "The Law of the Sea." *Oceanus,* winter 1982/83.

Goldwin, Robert A. "Locke and the Law of the Sea." *Commentary,* June, 1981.

Gordon, Bernard L., ed. *Man and the Sea: Classic Accounts of Marine Exploration.* Garden City, NY: Doubleday Natural History Press, 1972.

Grieves, Forest A. "Classical Writers of International Law and the Environment." *Environmental Affairs* 4, 1975.

Heath, G. Ross. "Manganese Nodules: Unanswered Questions." *Oceanus,* fall, 1982.

Henkin, Louis. *How Nations Behave.* New York: Columbia University Press, 1979.

————. "Politics and the Changing Law of the Sea." *Political Science Quarterly,* March, 1974.

Hildreth, Richard C., and Ralph W. Johnson. *Ocean and Coastal Law.* Englewood Cliffs, NJ: Prentice Hall, Inc., 1983.

Hollick, Ann L. *United States Foreign Policy and the Law of the Sea.* Princeton, NJ: Princeton University Press, 1981.

"King Crab Fishing Closed in Alaska." *New York Times,* October 3, 1983.

Knecht, Robert W. "Deep Seabed Mining Money—A Step Closer to Reality." *Ocean Science,* June 23, 1980.

————. "Introduction: Deep Ocean Mining." *Oceanus,* fall, 1982.

Knight, W. S. M. *The Life and Works of Hugo Grotius.* London: Sweet & Maxwell, Ltd., 1925.

Koh, Tommy T. B. "Should the United States Ratify the New Law of the Sea Treaty?" Lecture at Woods Hole Oceanographic Institution, Woods Hole, MA, June 4, 1980.

Koski, Randolph, et al. "Metal Sulfide Deposits on the Juan de Fuca Ridge." *Oceanus,* fall, 1982.

Lash, Joseph P. "I'm an Old Conservationist." *The Amicus Journal,* winter, 1983.

Malone, James L. "Law of Sea Policy." Speech at the University of Virginia, Center for Oceans Law and Policy, 7th Annual Seminar, Montego Bay, Jamaica, January 6, 1983.

————. *Ocean Policy and the Exclusive Economic Zone.* Washington, DC: U.S. State Department, 1983.

Marshall, Harry R. "Law of the Sea and the New U.S. Oceans Policy." *New York State Bar Journal*, April, 1983.

Murphy, Cecily. "LOS Preparatory Commission Begins Work." *Soundings*, May, 1983.

————. "Polymetallic Sulfides." *Soundings*, November 1981–February 1982.

National Oceanographic and Atmospheric Administration. *Deep Seabed Mining.* Washington, DC: U.S. Department of Commerce, March, 1981.

98th Congress, 1st Session. S. 750 Exclusive Economic Zone. Washington, DC: U.S. Government Printing Office, 1983.

Oxman, Bernard. H. "The New Law of the Sea." *American Bar Association Journal*, February, 1983.

Pardo, Arvid. *Official Records—Agenda Item #92.* New York: United Nations General Assembly, 22d session, November 1, 1967.

Pendley, William P. "The Argument: The U.S. Will Need Seabed Minerals." *Oceanus*, fall, 1982.

Ratiner, Leigh S. "The Law of the Sea: A Crossroads for American Foreign Policy." *Foreign Affairs*, summer, 1982.

Raymond, Nicholas. "Sea Law: The Unpleasant Options." *Ocean World*, January 1, 1978.

Reagan, (President) Ronald. "Convention on the Law of the Sea." *Weekly Compilation of Presidential Documents* 18:27, July 12, 1982.

Richardson, Elliot L. "Law of the Sea." *EPA Journal*, March, 1981.

————. "The Law of the Sea Treaty: The U.S. Should Reconsider." *Sierra Club Bulletin*, April/May, 1983.

————. "Power, Mobility and the Law of the Sea." *Foreign Affairs*, spring, 1980.

Ross, David A. "Marine Science and the Law." *EOS.* American Geophysical Union Transactions, September, 1981.

Safire, William. "The Old Order Changeth Not." *New York Times*, May 21, 1981.

Schachter, Oscar. *Sharing the World's Resources.* New York: Columbia University Press, 1977.

Seidel, Stephen, and Dale Keyes. *Can We Delay a Greenhouse Warming?* Washington, DC: U.S. Office of Policy and Resources Management, September, 1983.

Simon, Anne W. "To Rule the Waves." *Ekistics*, March/April, 1982.

Supreme Court of the U.S. *United States v. State of Maine et. al: Mr. Justice White*, March 17, 1975.

Swing, John Temple. "A Treaty for the Taking." *Oceans*, January, 1981.

United Nations Department of Public Information. *A Guide to the New Law of the Sea.* Reference Paper 81, March, 1979.

Vreeland, Hamilton. *Hugo Grotius: The Father of the Modern Science of International Law.* New York: Oxford University Press, 1917.

Wertenbaker, William. "The Law of the Sea." *New Yorker,* August 1, 1983; August 8, 1983.

Zuleta, Bernard. "The Law of the Sea: Myths and Realities." *Oceanus,* fall, 1982.

9. TRYING TO MANAGE
Pages 135 to 154.

Albion, Robert G.; William Baker, and Benjamin Labaree. *New England and the Sea.* Middletown, CT: Wesleyan University Press, 1972.

Apollonio, Spencer. "Fisheries Management." *Oceanus,* winter, 1982/83.

Armstrong, John M., and Peter Ryner. *Ocean Management—A New Perspective.* Ann Arbor, MI: Ann Arbor Science Publishers, 1981.

"Bass Fishermen Fear New Law Means Ruin." *New York Times,* November 14, 1983.

Becker, Margaret. *The 1982 Shellfish-Related Disease Outbreak in New York State: Agency Response and Interaction.* Albany, NY: New York Sea Grant Institute, February, 1983.

Belton, Thomas J.; Bruce E. Ruppel; and Keith Lockwood. *PCBs (Aroclor 1254) in Fish Tissues Throughout the State of New Jersey.* New Jersey Department of Environmental Protection, November, 1982.

"Bluefish Warning for Nursing Women." *Boston Globe,* September 10, 1983.

Conservation Law Foundation of New England. *Guide to Marine Fisheries Law.* Boston: October, 1980.

Crown, Eleanor H. "Traditional Chinese Ichthyology and Its Encounter with Jesuit Science: A Historical Survey." In Sears, M., and D. Merriman, eds., 1980.

"EPA Called Slow in Controlling PCBs." *Chemical and Engineering News,* January 18, 1982.

Farrington, John W., Edward D. Golberg, Robert W. Risebrough, John H. Martin, & Vaughan T. Bowen. "U.S. 'Mussel Watch' 1976–1978: An Overview of the Trace-Metal, DDE, PCB, Hydrocarbon and Artificial Radionuclide Data." *Environmental Science and Technology,* August, 1983.

Farrington, John W., B.W. Tripp, C. A. Davis & J. Sulanowski. "One View of the Role of Scientific Information in the Solution of Enviro-economic Problems." Proceedings of the International Symposium on Utilization of Coastal Ecosystems, Woods Hole Oceanographic Institution, Woods Hole, MA., November, 1982.

Gadbois, Don, and Richard S. Maney. "Survey of Polychlorinated Biphenyls in

Selected Finfish Species from United States Coastal Waters." *Fishery Bulletin* 81, 1983.

Hickey, J. Michael. "Assessment of Quahog Stocks in Contaminated Waters of Southeastern Massachusetts." Massachusetts Department of Fisheries, Wildlife and Recreational Vehicles—Division of Marine Fisheries, June, 1983.

Massachusetts Department of Public Health. *News,* November 3, 1983.

Melville, Herman. *Moby Dick.* New York: Penguin Books, 1978.

Menzies, Ian. "Fish Studies Public Matter." *Boston Globe,* August 25, 1983.

Miller, Marc, and John Van Naanen. "The Emerging Organization of Fisheries in the United States." *Coastal Zone Management Journal* 10:4, 1983.

New Bedford Area Chamber of Commerce. *The Yearbook,* 1982 ed. New Bedford, MA: New Bedford Area Chamber of Commerce, 1982.

National Marine Fisheries Service. *Annual NEMP Report on the Health of the Northeast Coastal Waters of the United States, 1981.* Northeast Monitoring Program. Woods Hole, MA: Northeast Fisheries Center, February, 1983.

————. *Calendar Year 1980 Report on the Implementation of the Magnuson Fisheries Conservation Management Act, 1976.* Washington, D.C.: U.S. Department of Commerce, 1981.

————. *Fisheries of the U.S., 1982.* National Oceanic and Atmospheric Administration. Washington, D.C: U.S. Department of Commerce, April, 1983.

————. *Status of the Fishery Resources off the Northeastern United States for 1981.* Woods Hole, MA: Northeast Fisheries Center, June, 1982.

National Oceanographic and Atmospheric Administration. "Status of the Fishery Resources off the Northeastern U.S. for 1982." Woods Hole, MA: Northeast Fisheries Center, June, 1983.

Radin, Charles A. "Mass. to Test Bluefish for PCB Contamination." *Boston Globe,* August 19, 1983.

————. "PCB Fear Has Blues Fishermen Wary." *Boston Globe,* August 21, 1983.

————. "Test of Mass. Bluefish Shows PCBs." *Boston Globe,* August 14, 1983.

Rehbock, Philip F. "The Victorian Aquarium in Ecological and Social Perspective." In Sears, M., and D. Merriman, eds., 1980.

Ridley, Nancy. Press release, Massachusetts Food & Drug Department of Health, November 5, 1983.

Sears, M., and D. Merriman, eds. *Oceanography: The Past.* Berlin, West Germany: Springer-Verlag, 1980.

Stutz, Bruce D. "Fishermen Seek Clearer PCB Rules." *New York Times,* October 23, 1983.

Thomas, Keith. *Man and the Natural World.* New York: Pantheon Books, 1983.

U.S. Environmental Protection Agency: *Environmental News Superfund Status Report.* September, 1983.

————. *Hazardous Waste Site Descriptions: National Priorities List Final Rule.* August, 1983.

————. *New Bedford Remedial Action Master Plan.* Final report, May 1, 1983.

————. *The Resource Conservation and Recovery Act—What It Is; How It Works.* September, 1983.

————. *Superfund: What It Is, How It Works.* April, 1983.

Weaver, Grant. *PCB Pollution in the New Bedford, Massachusetts Area: A Status Report.* Massachusetts Coastal Zone Management, June, 1982.

10. THE POSSIBILITY
Pages 155 to 174.

Alexandersson, Gunnar. *The Baltic Straits.* The Hague; Boston; London: Martin Nijhoff Publishers, 1982.

"Antarctic Minerals Regime." *ECO,* July 11–22, 1983.

Barnes, James N. "Last Chance for Wild Antarctic?" *The Living Wilderness,* June, 1979.

————. *Let's Save Antarctica.* Victoria, Australia: Greenhouse Publications, 1982.

————, Thomas C. Jackson, and Bruce Rich. *An Introduction to Southern Ocean Conservation Issues.* Washington, DC: Center for Environmental Education, 1980.

Bernstein, Richard. "UN Urges a Study of Antarctica." *New York Times,* December 1, 1983.

Bowman, Gerald. *Men of Antarctica.* New York: Fleet Publishing Corp., 1958.

Boxer, Baruch. "Mediterranean Pollution: Problem and Response." *Ocean Development and International Law Journal* 10:3/4, 1982.

Brown, William Y. "Comments of the Environmental Defense Fund." In U.S. State Department, no date.

Bunnell, Sterling. "The Evolution of Cetacean Intelligence." In McIntyre, J., 1974.

Costa, Daniel. "The Sea Otter: Its Interaction with Man." *Oceanus,* spring, 1978.

Cousteau, Jacques-Yves, and Philippe Diolé. *The Whale—Mighty Monarch of the Sea.* Garden City, NY: Doubleday & Co., Inc., 1972.

El-Sayed, Sayed Z., and Mary Alice McWhinnie. "Antarctic Krill: Protein of the Last Frontier." *Oceanus,* spring, 1979.

Friends of the Earth. "Antarctic World Park." *ECO,* January 17–28, 1983.

————. *The Whale Manual.* San Francisco; New York: London: Friends of the Earth, 1978.

Geraci, Joseph R. "The Enigma of Marine Mammal Strandings." *Oceanus,* spring, 1978.

Holdgate, Martin W.; Mohammed Kassas; and Gilbert F. White; eds. *The World Environment, 1970–1982—A Report by the United Nations Environment Programme.* New York: United Nations Environment Programme, 1982.

Holt, Sidney. "Changing Attitudes Towards Marine Mammals." *Oceanus*, spring, 1978.

"Hot Debate over the Frozen Continent." *Greenpeace Examiner*, fall, 1983.

International Institute for Environment and Development. *Antarctica—A Continent in Transition.* Washington, DC: International Institute for Environment and Development.

Jacobs, Myron. "The Whale Brain: Input and Behavior." In McIntyre, J., 1974.

Kearns, William H., Jr., and Beverly Britton. *The Silent Continent.* New York: Harper & Brothers, 1955.

Kessler, Anton. "For the Touch of a Whale." *Oceanus*, November, 1980.

Kimball, Lee. *Report on Antarctic Events: 1983.* Nottingham, England: International Institute for Environment and Development, 1983.

Langone, John. *Life at the Bottom—The People of Antarctica.* Boston, Toronto: Little, Brown & Co., 1977.

Lucas, Joseph, and Pamela Critch. *Life in the Oceans.* New York: E. P. Dutton & Co., 1974.

Marshall, Peter. "The Ways of Whales." In McIntyre, J., 1974.

Martin, Richard Mark. *Mammals of the Oceans.* New York: G. P. Putnam's Sons, 1977.

McElroy, James. "Krill—Still an Enigma." *Marine Policy*, July, 1982.

McHugh, J. L. "Rise and Fall of World Whaling: The Tragedy of the Commons Illustrated." *Journal of International Affairs* 31:1, 1977.

McIntyre, Joan. *Mind in the Waters.* New York: Charles Scribner's Sons, 1974.

McNally, Robert. *So Remorseless a Havoc.* Boston: Little, Brown & Co., 1981.

–––––––. "Sustenance for Cetaceans: Shortening the Food Chain." *Oceans*, March, 1981.

Melville, Herman. *Moby Dick.* New York: Penguin Books, 1978.

Mitchell, Barbara. *Frozen Stakes.* Nottingham, England: International Institute for Environment and Development, 1983.

–––––––, and Jon Tinker. *Antarctica and Its Resources.* London: An Earthscan Publication, 1980.

Mowat, Farley. "The Trapped Whale." In McIntyre, J., 1974.

National Marine Fisheries Service. *Marine Mammal Protection Act of 1972.* Annual Report, 1980/1981. Washington, DC: U.S. Department of Commerce, 1981.

National Research Council. *The Continuing Quest—Large Scale Ocean Science for the Future.* Washington, DC: National Academy of Sciences, 1979.

National Science Foundation. *Antarctic Conservation Act of 1978*. Washington, DC: National Science Foundation, 1979.

Neider, Charles, ed. *Antarctica*. New York: Random House, 1972.

———. *Beyond Cape Horn—Travels in the Antarctica*. San Francisco: Sierra Club Books, 1980.

Oceanic Society. *Marine Public Policy Program Proposal*. Stamford, CT: Oceanic Society, November, 1983.

Palacio, Francisco J. "The Cessation of Commercial Whaling." *Oceanus*, winter, 1982/83.

Parry, John. "Nations Unite to Fight Pollution." *Sea Frontiers*, May/June, 1983.

Report of the Southern Ocean Convention Workshop on Management of Antarctica Living Organisms. Washington, DC: Center for Environmental Education, 1980.

Riva, Joseph P., Jr., and James E. Mielke. *Polar Energy Resources Potential*. Report to the Subcommittee on Energy, Research, Development and Demonstration (Fossil Fuels), September, 1976.

Rosa, Nicholas. "Why Is a Whale." *Oceans*, March, 1981.

Ryan, Paul R. "Marine Mammals—A Guide for Readers." *Oceanus*, spring, 1978.

Saliba, Louis J. "Mediterranean Pollution Health Related Aspects." *Marine Policy*, April, 1983.

Scheffer, Victor B. *A Natural History of Marine Mammals*. New York: Charles Scribner's Sons, 1976.

"A School of Krill Measuring 10 Million Metric Tons." *Marine Fish Management*, April 19, 1981.

Shabecoff, Philip. "U.S. Presses Japan to Halt Its Whale Hunting." *New York Times*, January 2, 1984.

Sierra Club, International Earthcare Center. "Debate Over the Frozen Continent Heats Up." *International Report*, 1983/84.

Steele, John H. *An Evaluation of Antarctic Marine Ecosystem Research*. Washington, DC: National Academy Press, 1981.

Travalio, Gregory M., and Rebecca J. Clement. "International Protection of Marine Mammals." *Columbia Journal of Environmental Law*, spring, 1979.

United Nations Environmental Programme. *Achievements and Planned Development of UNEP's Regional Seas Programme and Comparable Programmes Sponsored by Other Bodies*. UNEP Regional Seas Reports and Studies, No. 1. New York: United Nations Environmental Programme, 1982.

———. *The Health of the Oceans*. UNEP Regional Seas Reports and Studies, No. 16. New York: United Nations Environmental Programme, 1982.

———. "Mercury and Microbes in the Med." *The Siren*, December, 1983.

United Nations Food and Agricultural Organization. *Mammals in the Seas*. Rome: United Nations Food and Agricultural Organization, 1978.

U.S. State Department. *Final Environmental Impact Statement on the Negotiation of an International Regime for Antarctic Mineral Resources*. Washington, DC: U.S. State Department, no date.

"Vast School of Krill." *New York Times*, March 14, 1981.

Victor, Paul-Émile. *Man and the Conquest of the Poles*. New York: Simon and Schuster, 1963.

Watt, Donald C. "Death of the Mediterranean." *Marine Policy*, October, 1982.

"Whaling Industry Sinking Fast." *Greenpeace Examiner*, fall, 1983.

Wolfe, Martha. "Who Should Rule the Ice?—Science in Antarctica May Be in Jeopardy." *Science News*, December 24 and 31, 1983.

11. PUT THE OCEAN FIRST
Pages 175 to 185.

Allen, Thomas B., and Norman Polmar. "The Silent Chase-Tracking Soviet Submarines." *New York Times Magazine*, January 1, 1984.

Botzum, John R. "A National Ocean Policy—Now!" *Ocean Science News*, March 30, 1981.

Bryne, John V. "The Year of the Ocean." Speech at Coastal Zone 83—Third Symposium on Coastal and Ocean Management, San Diego, CA, June 1, 1983.

Citizens for Ocean Law. *Ocean Policy News*. November, 1983.

Epting, John. "National Marine Sanctuary Program: Balancing Resource Protection with Multiple Use." *Houston Law Review*, July, 1981.

Knauss, John A. "Introduction: Marine Policy for the 1980s and Beyond." *Oceanus*, winter, 1982/83.

National Oceanic and Atmospheric Administration. *Status of the National Marine Sanctuary Program*. National Oceanic and Atmospheric Administration, December, 1983.

National Ocean Policy Roundtable. *First Meeting Materials*. Woods Hole, MA: Woods Hole Oceanographic Institution, 1983.

98th Congress. National Ocean Policy Commission Act of 1983—H.R. 2853. U.S. Government Printing Office, August 1, 1983.

Savage, Wayne. "Marine Sanctuary Site Recommendation." *Bulletin—The Coastal Society*, August, 1982.

"The Year of the Ocean." *Ocean Science News*, December 5, 1983.

211

Index

215

The Author

Anne W. Simon has written four books
to critical acclaim. She has examined
the degeneration of an island and of the
entire coastline, These studies led her
to present the formidable ocean in all
its dimensions. She has written a compelling book, using her journalist's skill,
her hard-earned understanding of the
sea, and her passionate crusading spirit.
The belief that man must start to act
with long-range perception is a lifetime
conviction, stronger in this book than
ever before.

A graduate of Smith College with a
master's degree from Columbia Uni-
versity, Anne Simon and her husband,
Walter Werner, Professor at Columbia
Law School, live in New York City and
Martha's Vineyard, Massachusetts.